Anne Russell and Patricia Fitzgibbons present speeches and seminars on the topics of Women and Leadership and The Roles of Women Today. Ms. Fitzgibbons is an educational specialist and Dr. Russell is completing a degree in law.

CAREER AND CONFLICT

A Woman's Guide to Making Life Choices

Anne Russell
Patricia Fitzgibbons

A SPECTRUM BOOK

PRENTICE-HALL, INC.
Englewood Cliffs, New Jersey 07632

Library of Congress Cataloging In Publication Data

Russell, Anne (Anne L.)
    Career and conflict.

    (A Spectrum Book)
    Includes bibliographical references and index.
    1. Women—Psychology.   2. Decision-making.   3. Choice
(Psychology)   4. Conflict (Psychology)   5. Women—Social
conditions.   I. Fitzgibbons, Patricia.   II. Title.
HQ1206.R79   305.4'2   81-12127
                             AACR2

ISBN 0-13-114512-6

ISBN 0-13-114504-5 (PBK.)

This Spectrum Book is available to businesses and organizations at a special discount when ordered in large quantities. For information, contact Prentice-Hall, Inc., General Book Marketing, Special Sales Division, Englewood Cliffs, N.J. 07632.

10 9 8 7 6 5 4 3 2 1

Printed in the United States of America

Editorial/production supervision and interior design by Frank Moorman
Manufacturing buyer: Cathie Lenard

305.42
R96c

Prentice-Hall International, Inc., *London*
Prentice-Hall of Australia Pty. Limited, *Sydney*
Prentice-Hall of Canada, Ltd., *Toronto*
Prentice-Hall of India Private Limited, *New Delhi*
Prentice-Hall of Japan, Inc., *Tokyo*
Prentice-Hall of Southeast Asia Pte. Ltd., *Singapore*
Whitehall Books Limited, *Wellington, New Zealand*

To my mother, a courageous woman who taught me how to try.

    PMF

To my father, who tried to encourage beyond tradition and to Dara, Canyn and Rebecca who shall look with open eyes toward the choices ahead in their lives.

    ALR

Contents

Preface

The idea for *Career and Conflict* developed from the experience of the authors, each set of which contributed to the total framework of the book. As the authors drew from their lives to develop the theme, they compared different life choices and the reasons behind those decisions which culminated in the direction of their own careers and family structure.

The authors feel this exploration of major decisions for women is a unique contribution to the field of literature, especially literature for women. The book deals with both the emotional and the practical sides of conflicts that stem from choices and have influence on a woman's career and family. Major life decisions are investigated in relation to career conflicts in an effort to clarify the inner struggles which women face. Real situations are presented which span age and socioeconomic divisions. The authors wish to share their own perspectives on conflict as well as to give examples of other women experiencing similar conflicts so that the reader may better understand the process of struggling with conflict. The authors provide a developmental structure for recognizing the conflicts which stem from choice. They hope that the clarification can help women and their supporters work through the conflicts related to the major life decisions of home and career.

The names used in the material contained in this book have been changed to protect the privacy of those interviewed.

CAREER
AND
CONFLICT

I
EVOLUTION
OF
CONFLICT

1
Changes in Traditional Roles

IN THE BEGINNING of life, each of us was supported, and cared for by the unquestioning love of a woman. This miraculous satisfaction borders on a bodly worship. We were hungry and were were fed; thirsty and were given drink. Each of us either subconsciously or otherwise realizes the very essence of our being relates to the ministering and comfort of a woman. The seed is planted in our minds that comfort and satisfaction are rooted in femaleness. The role of caretaker, nurturer of the universe, is one we all share through experiences. The glimmer of hidden memories nourishes our uncomfortable feelings about the shifting roles of women.

There have been many changes in the role of the woman. With the conveniences of modern society, housework requires less time. In olden times, women were somewhat more sure of their value than they are today. Women in many cases were necessary for the family to survive. They had to supervise the growing and preserving of the family food. They had a large number of children to raise. They had to make the family clothes. They had to make blankets, quilts, sweaters, soap, candles, and other household goods. The women were seen as the providers as well as the nurturers. With the development of industrialization and the smaller family, the child-rearing years and home-bound years of the female have been shortened and her domestic skills replaced.

Our societal equation in factoring the worth of an individual and the worth of his or her position clearly involves dollars. Until the priorities of our society are reordered, the most successful positions are in the areas of entertainment with special emphasis on sports. Society speaks clearly by the standards of monetary value which have been established. Sports and other forms of entertainment are more important in American society than the humane fields which nurture individuals and develop the mind. Traditionally, the low prestige fields of nurturing have been held by women, whose financial value has diminished because of the noble choice to cultivate ideas rather than muscles.

Human beings need a sense of worth. They need to feel that what they do is important and is valued on a real basis—not just through lip service. Men will say that being a wife and mother is a wonderful job, but it isn't worth money and it doesn't bring power or prestige in the eyes of society.

One's place in society is established by one's accomplishments—one's achievement. A woman's place has been directly associated with the achievement of her husband. Few women have been considered genuinely successful on their own. If women are to achieve and be respected for their accomplishments, they must do so in the man's world.

Several factors have helped to change social attitudes. The women's movement promoted the awareness of women's needs. Inflation created a situation that required in many cases dual family paychecks. Affirmative action legislation forced many companies to recruit women for jobs. These factors combined to shift social attitudes in the direction of acceptance and support of the career-motivated female.

Women themselves have begun to break down the traditional barriers concerning ambition that once stood in the way of their own success. Goal orientation, career planning, and the establishment of priorities are becoming acceptable. With the change in social attitudes, women have begun to express their inner career aspirations without fear of reprisal. Women are admitting their ambitious feelings.

The opinion that women work just for self-fulfillment and enrichment is outdated and inaccurate. Although at one time there may have been some basis for this assumption, it no longer holds true for the majority of American women. Women are working for financial survival. Just like men, most women work because they have to work.

Women whose backgrounds include highly motivated and successful parents are likely to be high achievers themselves. An open-minded attitude toward the professional expectations of all children in a family, regardless of their sex, encourages a girl to expect the most from herself. A female who is expected from childhood to attend college will develop an orientation in that direction. When parents encourage advanced training, they are in actuality encouraging high levels of attainment for their children. Parents are laying the foundation for the professional career development of their children. Their actions express their value system and communicate to their children the importance of a professional career. The children, as a result, will usually tend to incorporate these expressed values into their own.

Women have varying incentives behind their aspirations. Many women feel they have always been career-oriented. Others have acknowledged their desire to remain in the home and raise a family. For some women, the motives to work evolved from dreams of success and from ambition; for others, certain goals were expected to be achieved.

To resist patterns of expected behavior a woman has had to challenge the institution of tradition, a solidly long-standing foundation. In order to receive the applause of society, a woman must have proven beyond a doubt that she has fulfilled all her "expected" roles and devoted all her physical and psychological energies into the home. An achieving woman has had to risk the threat of societal scorn in order to pursue her "abnormal goals."

So it has been in the past and so it would remain without efforts to arrest the continuation of the restricting roles imposed by tradition. As society has slowly changed, the traditional roles of women have been altered, but the roots of tradition are strong and deep. Because of this, women have had to experience conflict in trying to balance their traditional roles with career goals.

Having been programmed with the notion that a man will marry a good little girl and take care of her for the rest of her life, some women spend their entire lives looking for a man and feeling that their fulfillment comes in providing service to men. Considering the divorce rate and outcome, the rewards to a compliant, subservient woman really do not match the promises of love and care forever.

More and more women have been faced with dissatisfaction over their "place" in man's world and have theorized that there is more to life than tradition has dictated. More women than ever in history have joined the labor market—many because they need to work and many because they need to increase their sense of independence.

Traditionally, decisions concerning marriage and children were rarely questioned or even acknowledged. Certain compromises were expected. The only problem with this legendary expectation was the limitation which these compromises brought to women.

HOW IT ALL BEGINS

Traditional roles for women have been developed and defined by society and do not overlap into those characteristics expected of men. An old rallying point against the assertiveness of women lies in the argument that the female character should possess mild and sensitive virtues rather than bold ones. In ancient times, it was considered alarming for a woman to create admiration rather than affection. A woman was in essence asked to choose which character she wanted to assume. Those women who have tried to combine masculine and feminine roles have been faced with stress and conflict.

The fantasyland romance meant that the man had only agreed to limit his naturally roving eye, whereas the woman, in return, provided him with a home and bed worthy of such sacrifice. He would then work hard to climb the ladder of success while she provided for his every need to support his adventurous maneuvers. Eventually, children were duly delivered, as expected, and again the woman took charge of her duties, as per tradition. Of course, in fantasyland, this ideal and peaceful arrangement functions well and continues to convince some that by striving for the ideal, they will eventually achieve it. However, fantasyland has no room for assumptions about human nature. The prince and princess of the castle have no economic needs that are not met. They have no emotional and psychological needs. There is no motivation for change in husband and wife roles because there is no reason for change. Seeds of discontent are not planted unless fulfillment is withdrawn.

Role definitions are limiting. They require certain patterns of behavior and restrict freedom to develop, to be yourself. Roles impose barriers on both sexes which must be followed in order to win approval from others and rewards from society. Dissension brings the risk of ridicule and the fear of failure.

Sex-role stereotyping begins at an early age, from the time babies are given pink and blue blankets in the hospital nursery. Remember the behavioral results of the newborn babies whose blankets were switched? Boy babies in pink blankets suddenly looked cute and pretty, and girl babies in blue blankets were perceived as potential football players.

Observance of behavioral differences are seen in preschoolers. Boys pull hair, smear food, and hit each other, whereas such behavior is never expected of girls. Usually such differences are explained on a cultural basis. Boys are expected to be more aggressive and play rough games, and girls are presumably encouraged to be gentle, nonassertive and passive. Girls hear their parents caution them time and time again to "be a little lady." After several years of exposure to such expectations, men and women wind up with behavioral expectations for the sexes. Many people believe that if childrearing practices could be equalized and sexual stereotypes eliminated, most of the differences would eventually disappear. Undoubtedly, many of the differences traditionally believed to exist between the sexes are based on stereotypes.

In the past, women have been educated for marriage. Their roles are defined from the beginning as little girls. Typically, girls orient their development toward charm and the seduction of a husband to fulfill the dream of living in the dollhouse. Many mothers of girls tend to think of college selection in terms of where to find the best husband—as a place to exchange the MISS for MRS degree.

CONDITIONING

Women have been conditioned since birth to focus their attention on the home to the exclusion of the development of any talents they may have. The cute little baby dolls of yesterday become the real-life babies of today. The doll buggy becomes the grown-up pram and stroller —symbols of attainment in the world of adulthood rather than fantasy and make-believe. Dollhouses are replaced by condominiums and houses to decorate, which beg for a woman's attention and pull at her for primary responsibility.

Those women who do tackle the challenge of the professional marketplace are faced with conflicts from many directions. The guardians of the marketplace question their credentials and motivation in a manner never even considered for male initiates in the work force.

Too many women translate their service image into the work force and cause a statistically skewed picture of women in fields of a service nature. They are not conditioned to look for work that interests them, work that is exciting and challenging.

The traits most often found in professional roles are traditionally considered masculine: aggressiveness, emotional detachment, independence, and persistence. Women have never been expected to possess such qualities, nor have they been taught how to handle them.

Until the crackdown on sex-role stereotyping in books, a mother was never shown working outside the home. A review of these books show her consistently wearing an apron over her dress and usually doing something in the kitchen. On her rare textbook outing, she is shown shopping at the local food market or buying new shoes for Dick and Jane. The readers of these books learned to shape themselves in that maternal role. The highlight of the primer stories focused on the arrival of Dad, home from his day at work. It was never even suggested that Mom might be coming home from work, much less that she might be a scientist or an executive.

Children derive their self-image from the culture in which they were raised. They learn what is expected of males and females. They develop a value system of rights and wrongs, likes and dislikes, and acceptable and unacceptable social behaviors. They learn what kind of work is of high value and what is considered low in value. This cultural conditioning usually affects decisions made later in life.

Two five-year-olds were playing. David, whose father was a doctor and whose mother was a housewife, said to Karen, "I'm going to be a doctor when I grow up. What are you going to be?" Karen hesitated only briefly before answering, "I'm going to be a doctor, too." David replied, "You can't be a doctor because you're a girl. Girls have to be nurses." Karen, seeming to be confident in her direction, retaliated, "Oh, no they don't. Girls can be doctors, too." Karen's mother was a professor and was seen by Karen as the image of strength and dependability.

Men, as boys, expect to grow up and support themselves and their families. Girls do not grow up thinking the same way. With the continuation of fantasies of motherhood and husbands having started in early childhood, girls grow up thinking that even if their mother works, the father's job is more critical. Few girls grow up thinking about working for the rest of their lives. They have to prove their seriousness and commitment.

Boys learn team play, how to use each other's strength and pull together. They learn how to tolerate each other. They learn that blockers and tacklers are as necessary as runners. Later on men use this knowledge and transfer it into the skills of planning and leading. They are bent on winning by survival, and they learn to work with men they wouldn't choose as friends. As boys, they learn to hide, to survive, to persist, and to win as a team.[1]

Perceptions about sex roles influence the personality development of boys and girls. Such traits as warmth, expressiveness, and sensitivity are considered feminine, whereas less emotional and more aggressive traits are associated with masculinity. Competence and femininity are not necessarily mutually exclusive. Some women even fear success because they associate achievement with forfeiture of the approval of society and those around them.

As children grow older, they see the mother as the physical provider of needs, from the bath to clothes and food. The role of the mother changes as the physical and social needs of children change. As the children learn to feed and dress themselves, the mother becomes the family facilitator of schedules, managing ball practices, ballet, music, swim lessons, and birthday party invitations. Mothers never fail to make sure that birthdays are good memories.

Society tends to assume that the woman as the center of the family is occupied by traditional domestic tasks, raising children and mistress of the hearth as ordained by nature. The woman is seen sitting by the fire, sewing or quilting, with little ones gathered around and the aroma of fresh bread escaping from the oven.

By remaining in this molded image, women may miss the surge of excitement in a whole new world in which they do not rely on men for their definition, either at home or in the work place. Many women are afraid to step into the working world because they have been programmed to be helpless. They have been taught that the true rewards of life come from service to others. In becoming self-reliant and competitive in the world of work, they lose their option to be dependent.

Many girls dream of being a mother, married to a successful business-man. They picture having two or three children who would be immaculately dressed at all times and a dog and cat who get along beautifully. These thoughts about the ideal family are again and again impressed upon the growing girl. She is even seen driving the station wagon with wood on the side and a luggage rack on the top for those memorialized family vacations with the perfectly behaved children. A manicured lawn with colorful

---

[1] Adapted from *The Managerial Woman* by Margaret Hennig and Anne Jardim. Copyright © 1976, 1977 by Margaret Hennig and Anne Jardim. Reprinted by permission of Doubleday & Company, Inc.

flowers, a fenced backyard for the children complete with the jungle gym and the red wagon, a basketball goal, bicycle, and sandbox—these substantiate the evidence of proper parenting.

Some mothers go through the act of taking time off from their roles and even boast about not feeling guilty on "my one day to myself." Imagine, one whole day to take a cooking course so that she can improve her motherly role. One whole day devoted to bargain shopping in efforts to help the strained family budget.

What about the stroking all human beings need? Where are the ego rewards? Women seldom realize how much they have done for others. Who says to a woman, "You did a good job as a mother today"? When does the raise come and what is the job title—Associate Director of Home and Family Service or Vice-President for Home Engineering? The equation does not work. For forty hours of work, a woman does not get forty hours of satisfaction, paid or otherwise.

"The monetary value of a homemaker was used as the basis for a divorce settlement which set a legal precedent. A Chicago attorney, Michael Minton, charted a line-by-line breakdown of his estimate for the worth of a homemaker. He compared the jobs a homemaker performed to the replacement cost of those jobs. For the varied tasks executed by a home-maker, the cost of her replacement set her value at $793.79 a week, or $41,277.08 annually."[2] Unfortunately, women do not receive just compensation for the services they are expected to perform. They seldom receive credit or appreciation for their work, though the benefits are enjoyed by many others.

PERPETUATION
OF MYTHS

There are many unstated myths about women, ranging from innately maternal, silly and unorganized, to dumb blonde. Several of these myths depict the dependent nature of a woman and her uselessness in the competitive work force. For example, women are supposed to enjoy cooking and loathe mathematics. What can be said for those poor women who, in all their unorganized state, run head on into a perfect marriage with calculus or chemistry?

The idea has long been perpetuated by philosophers such as Aristotle

[2]*Women USA*, August 1980.

that women do not have the brain power to compete with men. Though not originated by Aristotle, this theory was manifested through the following centuries, advocated by many, and used as an excuse to withhold education from women. Even in early America when education was primarily a spin-off of the church, girls were usually denied the right given freely to boys. When the first public school for girls in Boston opened in 1826, the response was so great the school soon closed its doors for fear it would "break" the city financially.[3]

Much research has been conducted on one of the most readily acceptable theories about women—that of women and math. The theory went that men were superior in math because of the ability to visualize shapes and mentally move or rotate them. In a two-year study reported in 1980 by the National Institute of Education, conducted by the Education Commission of the States, this myth was found to be false. Conversely, it was found that in the eighth grade, girls are actually better than boys at spatial visualization, and that by grade twelve, the skills were approximately equal. The end of this old myth is late in coming because math is one of the hurdles to be crossed by any woman who seeks a career in medicine, science, or engineering.

Girls continue to experience a strong conflict between academic achievement and popularity because they believe that boys do not like girls who excel in certain areas. In many cases, girls choose not to pursue certain fields such as math because it might hamper their social relationships with boys.

It has always been a struggle for women to be considered as having equal powers of the mind as men. Whereas contemporary feminists still fight for rights, laws, and open attitudes toward women, earlier feminists fought to disprove the myth that women cannot learn, reason, or compete. The principles upon which women have firmly stood revolve around the same interpretations of the broad potential of female ability. Women have gained a small degree of change and acceptance compared to other societal changes. The long road of tradition still remains to be traveled, but the narrow path which has been its course for years now finds crossroads at every bend.

---

[3] From *Education in a Free Society: An American History,* Second Edition, by S. Alexander Rippa. Copyright © 1967, 1971 by Longman Inc. Reprinted by permission of Longman Inc.

THE LEGACY

Men and women get a lot from their mothers: life sustainment, affection, worth. They also get a lot from their fathers: encouragement, respect, support. Elements of character development are shaped by influence from both parents, including views about marriage and family, parenting, and life priorities.

Growing up in a house where the father won't lift a finger forms behavioral patterns for the next generation. Sons who see this type of behavior believe it to characterize the father's role. When they become fathers they express the expectations developed in childhood.

Daughters who grow up seeing their mothers work only in the kitchen believe that is the behavior expected of them when they become mothers. They learn not to expect too much of fathers who "work all day and are tired at night."

The maternal legacy is delicate and, though unspoken, passed to daughters by mothers who herald the message of marriage, femininity, and babies. Many women who heard that message in childhood responded obediently and fulfilled their "maternal image," only to find later in life they were in search of their own identity. Some of those who went along with the expectations presented during childhood may have feared traveling the road of ambition alone if they turned down an appealing prospective companion. Then again, the fear of disappointing one's parents and family or straying too far away from the expected pathway may have demanded more courage at the time than young women were able to muster.

Women who clarify their identity early usually have less conflict than those who never seem to sort out the root of their feelings from their goals in life. Awareness of one's abilities and the drive and determination to nurture those abilities cause a woman to be more cautious in her decisions because she possesses some degree of knowledge about how that decision will fit into her life and the impact it may have on her plans.

One of the most important elements of the legacy from mother to daughter is the way in which the daughter sees the effect of a professional career on her mother. A female child can realize that for her, like her mother, a career is a possibility, an option open for her choosing. It is not a trade-off with womanhood. It is not antifeminine or antiparenthood. Women who work have the opportunity to share this testimony of the independence and satisfaction derived from developing a woman's skills at work. The effort is self-defeating if a working mother complains about hating her job and does nothing about changing it. Her positive example is also lost if she is remiss in the open acceptance of promotions and opportunities for greater amounts of responsibility. If she chooses a lesser course of action and, in effect, derails her career ascension because of tendencies against extra work, pressure, or family "duties," she repeats the negative model by her failure to advance.

Some of the realities of work can also be shared by working mothers if they are careful to explain the whys of each-situation. An explanation from a mother to a son or daughter can help the child understand why she is managing the home without support and working full time. Further understanding of the why behind the situation may result in inspired compromise or a dedicated determination to change restricted roles when the children reach adulthood.

Many relationships of later life are based on the legacies acquired throughout childhood. Some men are shattered when they marry to find their wives unwilling to pick up socks or arrange their clothes as mother did. These same men may have noticed mother delivering these services to father, and the expectation of nurturing and attention was well established. In many cases, the situation did not change whether mother worked or not. Thus, some boys saw mother, a professional career woman, accommodate the family without the traditional role of the father being altered in any way. As these boys grew to manhood and married, some found their marriages in turmoil as they struggled to work out problems of conflict perpetuated by traditional expectations.

Mothers who stayed home and gave no direction to their daughters often served as negative role models. Daughters saw their mothers grow out of shape and out of the mental limelight. As these mothers grew older, the daughters grew wiser and set their direction through admiration of their fathers. Much research has been done emphasizing the successful outcomes of a positive father-daughter relationship. Girls who were inspired and encouraged by their fathers experienced a range of feelings about their mothers as maids and felt a strong drive to disassociate themselves from that image. Others experienced feelings from mild affection to indifference. Still, daughters who were closer to their fathers tended to show more aggressive ambition than those who struggled to maintain femininity and image as a high priority.

Andrea was one such woman. Her mother had worked off and on during Andrea's childhood, but the work she did was not skilled or intellectual in nature and Andrea thought little about its importance. Her father owned his own store, and Andrea frequently accompanied him to oversee various responsibilities there. The relationship with her father, who was fortyish when Andrea was born, was always one of kind, loving encouragement. He took her to school and prompted her activities for the day with competitive words. Andrea responded with very good grades and became the ideal student. As Andrea grew older, she patterned her thinking after her father, whom she considered far superior to her mother in intelligence. Her mother became a strong motivation, but in reverse. More than anything else, Andrea did not want to grow up to be like her mother. She never felt strong conflict between ambition and a domestic image. She had made a choice early in her life.

Sons or daughters who do not develop definite role patterns for men and women are more able to use flexibility to meet the needs of their particular lifestyles. Seeing the father do household chores or laundry removes the negative connotation which causes men to refuse such tasks. Boys who see their fathers vacuuming are likely to accept responsibilities without embarrassment. Restricted models of men and women can be damaging to sons and daughters who transfer those limitations to adult life. They, in turn, lose freedom and mobility because the options to them are closed. Lessons of childhood immensely complicate the problems of adjustment and self-discovery in adulthood.

FACE TO FACE
WITH CONFLICT

Women are looked on as the reflection of the society they participate in rather than the creator of that society. Women are seen as the appendages of stronger men. The status quo tends to keep perpetuating itself, as a top continues to spin.

The traditional, natural, and age-old custom of woman's place being in the home has been accepted as if it were fact. Women were isolated from the work world and the marketplace and isolated from society.

A man has traditionally had two major sources of gratification, his family and his work, whereas a woman has only one, her family. If a male finds one of his roles unsatisfactory, he can frequently focus his interests and concerns on the other. In contrast, if a female finds her role unsatisfactory, she typically has no major alternate source of gratification.

Women have been assigned a role similar to that of children. In the power centers of society—business and politics—women are to be seen and not heard.

Many women prefer to be subordinate because they have been brought up to be that way. Habit and conditioning hold many women in their place. They are led to believe that submission and charm will get them more out of life than any other traits.

Some women think that there is prestige in not working, stating, "I don't have to work." This may be coupled with the thought, true or false, "I live with a successful man; therefore I am a success." Some women receive justification through this line of thought. It is difficult to admit that they are living vicariously rather than developing their own degree of ability. Some of these women who eventually "spread their wings" and gain employment may feel a self-conscious gratitude toward their husbands for helping them to maintain a career and family.

Economic conditions such as inflation have influenced many women to decide to work outside the home. These women work to allow their families to maintain their accustomed standard of living. This produces conflict in the face of the traditional views many hold in regard to women.

Some women, who may prefer homemaking, are forced into the working world by economic pressures. Mounting bills, financial responsibilities of children, and inflation have all contributed to the decision to work outside the home. Some women who work do so to maintain a way of life. Their particular standard of living requires more income than their husband brings home. The family expenses outstretch his paycheck. In these cases, women go to work to supplement the family budget. Their earnings supply the extra income so that the budget can keep up with the financial demands of the family's lifestyle.

The number of families in which both husband and wife work have increased. With inflation, most husbands needed help with bills, so many wives went out to work to help them. With the annual rate of inflation continually climbing, monthly living expenses can require both the husband and wife to contribute financially. Extra expenses such as club memberships, entertainment, lessons for children, tuition, and vacations can all contribute to the need for more money.

Emergencies can create a need for two paychecks. Such a situation can occur if a major appliance finally breaks down or substantial house repairs can no longer be delayed. Larger purchases, such as a new car, carpeting, or furniture, can create just enough of a budget crunch that the wife decides to find a job. Some wives have joined the labor market to qualify for and help meet the expenses of sizable investments, for example, buying a house. This type of expenditure can consume a considerable portion of the household operating account. Without the additional income that a wife's salary can provide, the new home may never be financially affordable. Banks and other financial institutions now include a wife's income in lending decisions. Barring other variables, a two-paycheck family has a better chance to qualify for a mortgage and to receive a higher amount for the mortgage than do one-paycheck families. The National Association of Home Builders reported that more than 47 percent of families who bought new homes in 1978 had two wage earners to meet the payments.[4]

Couples who make large investments, such as a house, for example, frequently become financially overextended and encounter much emotional conflict. Often, they are faced with a two-sided dilemma. One side of the conflict encompasses the need for material possessions—all the things money can buy. The other side engulfs a desire to live life for emotional satisfaction, independent of money, that is, wanting togetherness, time for one another, and time to start and raise a family. In reality these emotional needs are often put aside if both partners are required to work to pay for the financial obligations of the material goods. Couples, at times, may wish they had bought the smaller house, or the less expensive furniture or car. They discover after the fact that they are prioritizing their lives around their financial commitments.

The wife in this situation does not have a decision to work or not work. She has to work. Because both incomes are needed to meet monthly expenses, the couple becomes trapped in the two-paycheck cycle. They are unable to afford to shift to a one-paycheck family. Thus, the decision to have a child keeps getting delayed.

Throughout American history, women have always been an important contributing element to society. During the industrial period, the workplace shifted from the home to the factory, thus creating new occupations for women. Despite this, women remained in low-paying job levels. The traditional image of the female role was not challenged until the 1970s.

Women's place in society and home has limited the expansion of their roles. Prestige, responsibility, and public acclaim occur in domains which

---

[4]Caroline Bird, *The Two Paycheck Marriage,* Rawson Wade Publishers, Copyright © 1979, p. 12.

are typically male-dominated. Women have in the past not been chosen or allowed to enter these domains.

THE THREAT
IMPOSED BY CHANGE

Many men feel that women should enjoy deferring to the husband or other males. They believe this to be part of women's charm. Standing quietly aside while the men discuss issues is a socially acceptable custom for women.

Some men fear that women will not stop at equality. When women ask for equal status, men interpret this to be demand for dominance. On the contrary, women actually want control over their own lives and authority in the outside world equal to their abilities.

Now that women have the power via the pill to undermine the traditional role of eminent motherhood, men are sensing a loss of control over women. They can no longer hold women in the home unless the women want to be there. In the face of all these changes, men are fearful of the possible consequences of the independence of women.

The woman's intense involvement in the reproduction of human life has given rise to continued envy, awe, and dread. A traditional reaction to these emotions has been to view the female ability to create as innately superior to that of the male. Women have been led to believe that their bodily functions rightly establish the restrictive barriers for their roles in life. Many women now feel just the opposite, that their bodily capacities lock them into a physical and emotional prison. The body has become such a critical issue in the distinction of women that many have deliberately chosen to disenfranchise themselves from their physical attributes in order to become free in spirit; they refuse to be limited by their maternal bodily functions. Determined to separate mind and body, many contemporary women are redirecting the power inherent in female biology and determining that their biological destiny will no longer control the destiny of their life. For those unprepared to deal with such change, the freedom and independence of women is a real threat and difficult acknowledgment.

As more women are gaining financial independence through career opportunities, they are no longer dependent on men for financial survival. In the face of this additional threat, many men fear losing the traditional control they have held over women.

As myths of female weakness and vulnerability crumble, men find themselves competing with and being compared to women. To some, this is a fearful position, since according to tradition, losing to a woman is a difficult defeat to accept. As one man was recently overheard, "I think that men have been lucky to have had it so good for so long."

CHANGING SOCIAL CONDITIONS AND ATTITUDES

In recent years, attitudes concerning women's roles and issues have changed significantly. Social conditions surrounding the issues have also changed. As a result, women as a group have changed. They are having fewer children, marrying later, obtaining higher levels of education, and remaining in the work force longer. Women are working in jobs other than the traditional female stereotyped positions. Both internal and personal values and opinions and external social factors have contributed in the alteration of individual attitudes and social conditions. Thus, women have more opportunities than ever before to chart the course of their own lives.

New trends are altering established patterns of living. Women are remaining single longer and marrying later, divorcing and remaining single longer after the divorce, and having fewer children. These changes in women's life conditions have made women more available for the labor market. Because more women are on their own, employment is necessary for economic reasons.

The declining birth rate is another major trend that has affected women and the labor market. This trend has accounted for the increased availability of women who are able to work outside the home. The United States Census Bureau reported that although most young people do plan to have children, they expect relatively small families.[5]

Increased birth control and decreased fertility rates have an obvious effect on a woman's participation in the work force. Since women are better able to control fertility, they are delaying pregnancy and having fewer children. The time that had traditionally been spent in raising a family is now being spent at work outside the home.

Besides postponing children, women are consciously spacing children to fit into the most convenient time so as not to interrupt or harm a

[5]Randolph E. Schmid, "One Parent Families Reported Up 80%," The *Associated Press*, August 18, 1980.

career. Women who time their children closer together are able to return to work sooner than women who have children over the time span of several years.

Large numbers of mature women whose families have grown are entering the labor force. The activities that were necessary when they raised children are no longer needed. They find extra time on their hands. Some women feel that they lose their purpose when their youngest child is grown. These women encounter the empty-nest syndrome. Their feelings of worthlessness are at times compounded by the actions of their husband. He is probably reaching the peak of his career and is heavily involved in his work. When she is feeling useless, he may be at the most productive time of his life. This only makes her feel worse. For most of her adult life she had been doing something for others or supporting the achievements of others. Some women will not have the need to establish their own identity or allow themselves to experience achievements until their "mothering" responsibilities have been completed. Others begin their upward struggle by channeling their unused energy into new avenues. Some women choose to develop their talents into hobbies and remain full-time homemakers. Other women have chosen to seek additional training and/or employment outside the home in order to fill time and utilize energy and skills.

Housewives have also found extra time on their hands. Although a family may not be totally grown and the children may be in school, many housewives are choosing to spend their time in different ways. Labor-saving household devices have freed women from the toils and rugged chores of yesterday. The electric dishwasher has cut meal clean-up time in half. The microwave oven and advent of frozen foods have cut down the time necessary for meal preparation. Advanced cleaning products have also made many chores quicker and easier. All these inventions, devices, and products combined have allowed the homemaker more time to spend with her family and for herself. Many homemakers are deciding to spend that time working outside the home.

Other changes have occurred which have directly affected women and work. Rising educational levels and expanding job opportunities have opened doors of employment for many women. These expanded opportunities lie in the areas of educational training and nontraditional job openings.

American women have always been a vital part of the labor force. In 1920, approximately 20 percent of the work force was female, and by 1978, the percentage climbed to 42. The later percentage constituted almost 50 percent of all women sixteen years and older.[6] The trend toward women working outside the home began building in the 1950s and exploding by the 1970s. The factors which account for the significant increase of women entering and remaining in the world of work are varied: they include changes in social attitudes toward working women, declining birth rates, increasing divorce rates, and the increase of single women. Still other factors have been the increase in jobs open to women, achievement of higher educational levels, and the longer life expectancy of women.

The profile of the average woman worker has changed greatly—from that of the twenty-eight-year-old single factory worker or clerk of the 1920s to that of the thirty-five year old woman of today who may be found in any of a great number of occupations.[7]

Women with families, as well as single or childfree women, work for many of the same reasons. Women and men also have similar motives to work. Women work because of economic conditions.

RECENT TRENDS

Millions of women, directly and indirectly, through dedication and commitment have made an increasingly effective impact on changing social attitudes and the recognition of restraining stereotypes that have kept American women from equal visibility and respect. Equality has been and will continue to be an issue in the decades to come as only the tip of the iceberg of equalization has been seen. Women are seeking fulfillment through choice in the family circle and work outside the home. Much has been done to reduce blockading barriers of social and economic achievement for women. Yet more, much more, remains to be done.

Women are beginning to realize and appreciate their own potential. They are focusing on long-range plans as well as intermediate goals to develop their abilities. They are saying to themselves, "Where do I want to go with my professional life, and what do I have to do to get there." They are permitting themselves to think in terms of a career for now and for the future rather than just a job for the here and now.

---

[6]*Women's Action Almanac*, ed. Jane Williamson, Diane Winston, and Wanda Wooten (New York: William Morrow, 1979), p. 80.

[7]Information from the Women's Bureau, U.S. Department of Labor, February 1981.

Women are beginning to have choices. They are beginning to realize that they have a choice to be single and professional; to marry and pursue domestic life; to marry and be involved in the community; to marry and have a job; and slowly but surely, to combine marriage and family with a profession.

The old fairy-tale bubble has burst. Susan now finishes college instead of dropping out to marry Howard. And with degrees in hand, she opts to work for a time before "settling down," instead of bearing her all-American son and daughter during this period in her life. Instead of buying that suburban ranch house, Susan is now buying a city condominium independently. Instead of changing diapers and scraping applesauce off the wall, Susan is now climbing the career ladder of her company. Instead of saving for private school tuition for the children and driving daily carpools to kindergarten and piano lessons, Susan makes her own decisions to buy designer clothes and travel. When Susan marries, she's not twenty anymore, and when she decides to have children, if she does, she may do so in her thirties.

A woman faces a decision in whether to begin a career that inevitably will involve her in conflicts with traditional images from imposed roles and her own expectations of fulfillment. Once this decision is made she may be forced again and again to review it as successive conflicts arise between her career and her personal life. She has to identify her goals and set her course accordingly, which may include aspiring for high rewards and power, as men have learned to do naturally.

Women are demanding more out of life. They want the same pleasures and rewards that have been unconditionally afforded to men. Women want to develop their yet untapped resources and abilities. Many are expecting to be admitted into the professional world. At the same time, some question traditional expectations that will sooner or later cause conflict with their career. Discriminating attitudes continue to produce professional and personal hardships for women. In response, women are working even harder to prove their worth and to receive recognition for their talents.

Women have the same life choices that men have had as part of tradition. In understanding and accepting those choices, women are building a future of less conflict for those of the next generation. In the past, women largely underestimated their capabilities, putting self-imposed barriers in the way of future employment possibilities. They rarely envisioned themselves as permanent members of the labor force. Women viewed work as a temporary situation with short-term objectives rather than long-range goals for a permanent career.

Women are developing their careers. They want a career for self-fulfillment and the realization of needs. Women have also began to pursue careers for tangible rewards. They have allowed themselves to admit that a career can bring forth material as well as emotional benefits. Up to this point, women have barely scratched the surface in their pursuit of career gratification.

Women are entering a new era. They are expecting more from themselves besides the traditional reinforcement of self-fulfillment. Women are venturing to demand as men have for years recognition and rewards.

II
CAREER

2

The Decision: Single or Married?

THE COMPOSITION of the American family has significantly changed in the last two decades. Several years ago, the ideal family consisted of a married couple with at least one or two children, and usually more. The father was the principle wage earner and head of the household, and the mother was a full-time homemaker. By the late seventies, only 15 percent of the families in the United States fell into this category.[1]

The altered family structure can be attributed to changes in social conditions. The upheaval and years of protest in the 1960s laid the foundation for the era of self-awareness in the 1970s. In the 1960s, the establishment was challenged. College students protested against the Vietnam war. Blacks struck out against prejudicial injustices. Social norms were no longer accepted as the way of life. People were beginning to speak out for what they believed in, even if it meant going against the established way. After the upheaval of the 1960s settled down, a new era of self-sufficiency and independence began. In the 1970s, people wanted to explore their own needs and enhance their capabilities. As a result, a more permissive society began to emerge. Social attitudes concerning family living patterns became less rigid. Adverse prejudices toward divorced and single people decreased. The effect was a greater acceptance of individual lifestyles. By the end of the 1970s, more individuals were choosing to remain single. For

---

[1] Information from *U.S. Statistical Abstract*, 1977.

those already in marriages, there were more numbers who chose to divorce. there was also a rise in the number of people who outlived their spouses. The end of the 1970s also brought an increase in the number of people who waited longer to get married and who failed to remarry after a divorce.

THE CHOICE:
SINGLE LIFE

The rapid increase of the single population was encouraged by sources other than social attitudinal changes. These sources included media channels, such as television and literature, and pressure from investors encouraging singles to become a part of the "good life." A new industry developed. Singles clubs began. People were influenced by the glorification of the single life to spend their money for health and sporting clubs, singles clubs, and beautification clinics so that they could be part of the new society. Even singles dating services and apartment complexes developed. Singles were encouraged to spend their money on themselves, buy more clothing, take vacations, eat in restaurants rather than cooking at home, and get involved in activities that would give them the opportunity to meet other single individuals. Because many single individuals do not have family responsibilities, they are free to spend more money on themselves. This motivated investors to encourage the singles industry even more. The women's liberation movement of the 1960s and early 1970s was a contributing factor to the increase in the single population. In the 1960s women began to see themselves as individuals. Antidiscrimination laws and lawsuits laid the foundation for future gains in women's individual rights. The 1970s brought forth new credit laws, housing advances, and more opportunities for educational training for women. The effects of the women's liberation movement created opportunities for women, first, to realize that they have capabilities, and second, to take advantage of situations that will develop their capabilities. Women were beginning to realize that they no longer had to get married or stay married for social acceptance and survival. Thus, two outcomes resulting from the women's liberation movement were that women recognized they had a choice to remain single and that job opportunities were made available for financial independence. The choice to remain single finally became a realistic option.

The Single Population

What is the single population and who is a part of it? There is a wide misconception concerning the nature of the single population. People assume that the typical single person is a career person in his or her late twenties or thirties who has a glamorous, responsibility-free life. In fact, the singles population includes many different types of individuals. In general, singles are those people who have never married, those who are divorced or separated and have not remarried, and those whose spouses have died. Some people who are single choose to remain single. Others are delaying marriage for various reasons but intend to marry in the future. In essence, single individuals cross socioeconomic lines, age categories, and cultural backgrounds. Simply stated, the single population consists of those individuals not living with a legal spouse.

There are many different perspectives concerning single life. To some, single life is a means of expressing individuality and independence. Single women often remark that they have continuous opportunities to develop potential for personal growth. They have been forced to rely only on themselves for emotional support, and as a result, have increased their self-esteem. They are not in a position that demands compromise. They can make their own decisions, either daily insignificant ones or major life choices.

Some women have a strong need for financial independence. They want to fulfill their own needs for self-respect through their earning power. Women who express this view usually do not want to depend on someone else for financial security. Inherent in this viewpoint is the concept that single life means establishing identity and freedom. A single female supporting herself financially can utilize her career to provide an opportunity for self-reliance and independence.

Single life may be a temporary status. Some women are either waiting to find the right person or between marriages. They are longing to be "unsingle." They equate being single with loneliness. Many have not been able to identify their personal growth nor develop the self-confidence to appreciate their own worth.

From 1971 to 1980, the number of single persons in the United States increased by 26 pecent.[2] In 1971, there were 43.8 million persons identified as single. By 1979, there were 55.8 million. From 1960 to 1978,

[2] J.L. Barkas, *Single in America* (New York: Atheneum, 1980), p. 15.

the percentage of population between eighteen and twenty-four remaining single rose by 43 percent for males and 40 percent for females. Although the increase was not as high among those 25 to 29, there was still an increase in the number of persons who remained single.[3]

The Widow

Widows are the largest component of single individuals in the United States. Nearly 20 percent of persons in the United States are single because of the death of a spouse. Of the nearly 56 million single individuals, 10.5 million are widows and 2 million are widowers. In the United States, one out of every six women over the age of twenty-six is a widow.[4] Of widows aged sixteen through forty-four, 51 percent have jobs outside the home. An older widow is less likely to work because of the social attitudes against a woman when she was younger. Many missed the opportunities to develop marketable skills. There still is, however, a substantial number of widows who work and who maintain their own support.

Statistics indicate that most American women will face widowhood. The rationale for this expectation can be attributed to the longer life expectancy for women and the "marrying up/marrying down" syndrome. The life expectancy for women is on the average four years longer than for men. The traditional tendency of women to want men who are older, more successful, and better educated than they, while men want just the reverse, is the "marrying up/marrying down" syndrome. This further increases the age difference between the husband and wife and increases the chances that the wife will be a widow some day. Besides awareness of insurance and wills, more women should be encouraged to prepare for the financial side of widowhood by either obtaining specialized training and/or entering the work force prior to the death of a spouse. In this way, a widow, no matter what her age, can be self-sustaining.

Sara, sixty-three, entered the work force prior to the death of her husband, and as a result, she is now financially independent. Sara recalled that, in her twenties, she felt very torn between her budding career and her decision to marry:

My future husband told me that no wife of his would ever work—he would not allow it. So I did what I thought I was supposed to do....

[3]*Ibid.*, p. 30.
[4]*Ibid.*, p. 97.

look back, I feel I wasted many years that could have been in career development.

Sara decided to reenter the work force after twenty-eight years. She was fifty-one years old, and her youngest child was seven and in the second grade. Her primary motive to securing employment was based on financial reasons. She also noted that she felt useless at home since her older children were grown and her youngest were in school.

With the help of a friend, she obtained employment with a temporary service as a clerical accountant and bookkeeper. After a year and a half at the same company as a temporary, Sara requested, fought for, and obtained a full-time position. Within the past five years, she has been promoted to an accountant with managerial status.

When she was fifty-eight, her husband died. She felt that her job not only provided financial security, but also provided a built-in structure to her life. Originally, she had returned to work after almost thirty years of homemaking to help the family budget, but she feels that, through her job, she has avoided becoming lonely, depressed, or displaced. She also feels that her career has afforded her the opportunity to develop her self-esteem, creativity, and has enabled her to reach her goal of financial independence.

Just like Sara, more and more women are going back to work after years of homemaking. Women have been increasing steadily in the labor market over the past thirty years and more rapidly in the last decade. Because of divorce, widowhood, and the choice to marry later or remain single, more women are the primary breadwinners in their families. They are providing their own financial support.

Divorced Women

The rise in the divorce rate and women's choice to remain single for longer periods of time after a divorce has paralleled the increased participation of women in the work force.

Most women who are single through divorce work to sustain their financial support and independence. A report from the United States Department of Health and Human Services, issued in 1980, disclosed that the nation's divorce rate is continuing to climb. The percentage of single women who are divorced and maintain a family rose over 30 percent from

1970 to 1980.[5] Only 14 percent of divorced women obtain alimony and fewer than one-half of those collect it regularly.[6] The other 86 percent depend on their own resources for support.

The once popular notion that a divorced woman has the life of ease, while the ex-husband labors two or three jobs to pay his expenses as well as hers, has little substance. Most divorced women depend on their own resources for financial survival and stability. Divorced mothers have more financial responsibilities than single women. Not only does a divorced mother have to provide for herself, but statistics show that in most cases she also has to provide the major portion of the financial support for her children. In nine out of ten cases the mother is given custody of the children, and she is likely to receive little or no child support from her ex-husband.[7] When child support is collected, it is often irregular and not commensurate with actual childcare costs. Divorced mothers find themselves in the position of having to be the breadwinner for themselves and their children. In effect they are assuming the traditional role of men as well as their own role expectations.

Marsha, a divorced mother of two children, realized quickly after her divorce that she was, and would be in the future, the major provider for herself and her children. Marsha was a secretary until the birth of her first child. She quit work to care for her child and after a year, she and her husband decided to have a second baby. When she was divorced, she discovered that although she could easily find a secretarial position, the salary would not provide enough income to meet all her expenses. She decided to move herself and her two daughters in with her parents. During that time she went to school to train in computer programming. With the additional training, she was able to get a job with a salary range within which she and her two children could live. As frequently happens, the child support that was awarded was insufficient to meet the expenses of raising the children. In addition, her ex-husband was inconsistent and irregular with the child

---

[5]Randolph E. Schmid, "One Parent Families Reported Up 80%," The Associated Press, August 18, 1980.

[6]Women's Action Almanac, ed. Jane Williamson, Diane Winston, and Wanda Wooten (New York: William Morrow, 1979), p. 77.

[7]Ibid., p. 52.

support payments so that she learned not to depend on his check for basic needs. She is providing the main source of financial support for her family. She stated that she missed the flexibility she once had to go to school functions for her children and be home when they arrived from school. Realistically she knows that she is able to furnish an adequate life for her children because of her job.

The Displaced Homemaker

Women in their middle years who have devoted their lives to raising children and homemaking and who are either unemployed or having difficulty in securing employment are displaced homemakers. A woman is usually displaced through widowhood or divorce. Displaced homemakers are without employment because their earlier years have been spent in homemaking rather than in career training.

In 1979 there were an estimated three and one-half million displaced homemakers in the United States. Title III of the Comprehensive Employment and Training Act provided that financial assistance be available to conduct programs to provide employment opportunities and appropriate training and support services to displaced homemakers.[8] Displaced homemakers and mature women seeking to enter the job market need job counseling, vocational training, and education. Networks such as The Displaced Homemakers Network in Washington, D.C. have been developed across the country to help older women seek employment.

Remaining Single

J.L. Barkas in *Single in America* reported three primary reasons for remaining single: commitment to career, independence, and not having met the right person.[9]

Many women are single because they feel that they have not met "Mr. Right." They are looking for the perfect man to come along. They hope to fulfill all their criteria for perfection before they make any long-term commitments. Some envision that one day they will encounter the ideal man who meets their needs and standards. Women who have a preconception of exactly what they want in a man may fail to perceive many traits, such as kindness and honesty, in men they meet. Because of their desire to have the perfect man they may lose track of the important

[8]*Ibid.*, p. 76.
[9]Barkas, p. 24.

characteristics which enrich a relationship. The concept of Mr. Right is encouraged by magazines, television, fairy tales, programs and advertisements. The attractive, intelligent, caring man is often put forth as the hero in the television programs or at the movies. Or he may be shown as Prince Charming to girls growing up. Magazine articles and advertisements encourage this by showing women with perfect-looking men. Thus, some women develop an image of a Mr. Right. Until he comes along, the search continues.

Many women have remained single or postponed marriage to pursue their career goals. In essence, they are satisfying their need for achievement and attainment of success. These women have expressed the opinion that a relationship that included a permanent commitment may hinder their career advancement. They want to be free of the roadblock to their career success. A marriage can make promotional transfers out of the question or put a squeeze on evening and weekend meetings and work. Goal-oriented women often place their long-range career goals above their personal lives.

Women often experience conflict when they are in a position to choose between career advancement and marriage. As men have done for years, women are beginning to integrate goals for their personal lives with their professional lives. Many women such as Caroline have made their careers a priority in their life. Caroline, who is in her early thirties, is involved in a promising career in television communications. She is successful because she has devoted long hours and much hard work to her career. She feels that her career has provided a framework by which she has been able to express herself and her abilities. She has the opportunity to demonstrate her creativity which is .rewarding to her personally. Caroline feels that she has gained the personal freedom of self-expression from her career outlet. She possessed a personal awareness which has enabled her to plan a life to fulfill her own needs. As a result, she has been able to enjoy the freedom inherent in a single life, and she has devoted her pursuits to career development and advancement. She does not see marriage as a part of her future life. Realistically her career involves a lot of travel and unpredictable hours, and she feels that she would not have the time to devote to a permanent relationship. She is also afraid that marriage may stifle or block her career through restrictive demands. She does not want to risk lowering the amount of freedom and satisfaction she derives from her career.

Some women believe that their independence may be jeopardized if they marry. They like planning their own schedules. They come and go as they please and choose the work and leisure activities that are most enjoyable. One woman stated that her motive to remain single is to keep her independent way of life. She feels that although there are lonely moments, she is in control of what she does. She feels that her identity might be absorbed by another person if she were to marry. At present, she is content with the status quo in making decisions for herself.

At times, women have remained single because of a rejection of traditional expectations. These women have rejected marriage in reaction to strong parental presumptions that they will marry. Women who feel a need to go against the grain of tradition and not marry place a great deal of importance on their career. They often feel that their career is their means to maintain personal freedom and to live their life as desired. They feel that their job has given them the means to remain independent of another's control. Thus, in return they can experience and keep their freedom.

Women have also expressed the desire to remain single because of the fear of making a mistake. Often, divorced women are especially leary of second marriages. Occasionally, negative experiences in previous relationships can cause a woman to be very cautious the next time around.

Some women have declined marriage opportunities because of educational commitments. Women in college or postgraduate work often do not feel that they have the time or energy to put into a serious relationship. Their educational goals come first, and they postpone ideas of marriage or commitments until their program is complete.

The Changing Image

The rise of the singles culture has had far reaching effects for the American woman. Alternative lifestyles that were once unthinkable are now realistic options. In the past, young adults took their futures for granted. They assumed that they would marry after their education was completed. Assumptions established the roles of both the wife and the husband in the family. The wife stayed home to raise the family, and the husband worked outside the home to provide financial support. Male and female roles and expectations became well defined.

However, the traditional family composition began to change and different living patterns evolved. Factors which contributed to the changes in family lifestyles were the woman's movement, advances in birth control, and more open social attitudes. Twenty years ago women who were single were thought of as old maids or spinsters. Socially, they were abnormal. The consensus was that the reason they never married was because no man would have them. They were at times estranged from social events and gatherings, for the host or hostess never wanted a fifth wheel or odd number. Unmarried women were assumed to be unhappy in their lifestyle and thought of as being lonely. Single women were social outcasts to be pitied.

This misconception has changed. Prior conditioning contributed to society's perspective that single people are unhappy and lonely. With the advent of the single culture, many of these myths have been dispelled. Recently, women have begun to experience the phenomenon of the respected and envied single female. New successful female role models have emerged to create a positive image of the single female. Women have begun to identify the benefits of single life and independence. They have begun to experience a new freedom and a higher degree of self-esteem. These feelings have been transferred into the professional life of many women. They no longer have to acquire the "Mrs." status for financial support. Because of the income earned by working, more women are able to maintain an adequate standard of living for themselves. Women who live in their own apartments or homes are not viewed with negative connotations. In the past, women lived at home with their parents until they married. Single females are no longer thought to be immoral or socially deviant if they live alone. Single women are at times envied by their married friends. There has been a shift from the old-maid perception to a view that the single way of life is glamorous and exciting. With this perspective, single women are viewed as being socially in demand rather than outcast.

Their lives are at times envied. They are not tied down with childcare responsibilities. They do not have to arrange their schedules around a husband's needs. They are independent to pursue personal and career objectives without family conflicts.

The lessening of social taboos on divorce has been a contributing factor in the increase of the rate of divorce, and thus, an increase in the number of single women. Divorced women now have an easier time emptionally as they try to blend into a couple-oriented society. Being alone is not treated in the negative sense it once was. Being divorced and alone no longer has negative connotations.

Divorced women are no longer thought of as losers. In fact, this concept has been turned around. More divorced mothers are now perceived in positive way. They have been able to release themselves from an unre-warding relationship and have begun anew. They have shifted from the loser's side to the winner's circle. Divorced women often find life alone to be difficult. If they had previously lived in a household with two pay-checks, they often have to adjust financially to a lower income level. Some women feel that they have given up emotional and marital problems for money problems. Other divorced women feel that the independence they have experienced with their financial budget has been rewarding. For the first time in their lives, they know what their money is spent on, and they can prioritize their own needs and their own budgets.

Many divorced women struggle with their social life. They may find dating difficult, yet they do not enjoy going out alone. They may also find that they cannot afford to go to certain activities, since the cost of tickets may strain their budget.

Women who are widowed may also realize that they are restricted financially and at times socially. The woman whose spouse has died may not want to go to activities alone, after years of going with her husband. The widowed woman today has more opportunities for a new life than ever before. The once prevalent notion that widows were to be pitied has evolved into the idea that widowed women can be productive. New career and educational opportunities are opening for the woman whose spouse has died. She no longer has to sit home and think of past memories. She is able to make new memories for herself.

The concept of marriage has evolved from a predictable eventuality to a choice. Both advantages and disadvantages are considered before making the decision to marry. Women are examining the long-range impact of marriage on their entire life. Not only are they looking at marriage in terms of their personal expectations, but they are appraising the effects of marriage on their professional goals. Women have realized that they have a definite choice to marry or remain single, and they are taking the time to make that choice. The freedom to decide whether or not to marry has created a responsibility to identify the consequences of each decision on the desired goals and lifestyle of women.

THE CHOICE:
MARRIAGE

The American culture places a great amount of importance on the institution of marriage. Although the American family has been somewhat altered in the past few decades, marriage is still a high priority.

A 1975 Market Opinion Research Study reported that 85 percent of women in the United States have been married at some time in their lives.[10] The 1980 Virginia Slim poll reported that 96 percent of people interviewed preferred marriage as a way of life.[11] American customs advanced marriage as the principle means to continue the society. Marriage is the primary means through which future generations are born, and despite the dramatic changes that have occurred in marriages, marriage has endured as a viable part of our society.

Our society expects its members to marry. Social life, public or private, has been oriented to the married couple. Clubs advocate family membership and family outings. Businesses have social events that include the spouses. Even the airline companies give discounts for spouses. As a result, many couples marry because of social expectations. Pressure from family members, business associates, and peers often contribute to the decision to marry. Parents may want grandchildren. Friends may be married and encourage their unmarried friends to join the ranks. Business associates may indirectly approach the issue with future promotional opportunities for the established and stable married worker.

People have married to gain adult status. These individuals often feel they demonstrate maturity through marriage and obtain social recognition as a part of the adult community. For some, marriage is a way to feel acceptance in a couple-oriented society. They are finally able to socialize with other married couples on an equal basis.

The desire for security has prompted many singles to want to marry. Both the man and woman may want a home and children. They want companionship and a lasting, dependable relationship. In essence, they are seeking security in an emotional relationship for the future.

Many people marry because they want children. The desire to have children can originate from an emotional need. Marriage provides a socially acceptable framework to accomplish this goal.

Others have married out of convenience. Marriage provides an acceptable excuse to stop dating. Marriage can become an escape from singlehood rather than an entrance into a shared relationship.

For younger adults, marriage has been a release from an unpleasant

---

[10] Barbara Everitt Bryant, *American Women Today and Tomorrow* (Market Opinion Research), National Commission on the Observance of International Women's Year (Washington, D.C.: U.S. Government Printing Office, 1977), 0-241-113(1), p. 21.

[11] Barkas, p. 28.

home situation. They desire to have independence from parental domination. These people feel that they are able to break loose from the control of their parents and establish their own identity through an established adult procedure—marriage.

Fortunately, many people marry for love. They experience feelings of pleasure and security as a result of the relationship with the other person. They desire and receive comfort, support, respect, and care from the other. Love, companionship, security, social approval, and stability, whether emotional or financial, have consistently remained the primary reasons to marry.

Changes
in Traditional Expectations

There has, however, been a recent trend de-emphasizing certain past reasons to marry. With the advent and widespread use of birth control methods, especially the pill, fewer marriages are caused by accidental pregnancies. Women have also become more aware of their own capabilities to take care of themselves. Hence, fewer women than ever before are marrying for the traditional "I want to be taken care of" option. Since more women are in the work force, they are now able to provide for themselves financially and no longer have to depend on a man for support.

Aspects of social change can be reflected through change in marital behaviors. This has happened in the American social system. Marriages have endured many changes in the shift from the traditional to the contemporary marriage. In the traditional marriage, the husband maintained a position of dominance and was the primary wage earner. The wife was expected to be viewed as dependent and helpless. The husband made all the major decisions. The main function of the wife was childcare and the maintenance of a comfortable atmosphere at home. The husband, on the other hand, advanced his career outside of the home and assumed his family would rearrange their lives when necessary.

The assumptions of marital patterns have shifted tremendously. Contemporary marriages are equated to partnership in which each partner is perceived with equal value and worth. Dominance by one spouse is no longer acceptable. Both individuals are seen to possess qualities that equally contribute to the good of the union.

In the past, when two people married, certain concessions were presumed. The man was expected to devote most of his time for the financial support of his wife and children. The wife was expected to care for the house, have children, and remain in the home to raise them. However, a great number of women have not remained in the home. They are having fewer children and are expecting shared responsibility for childcare and household chores.

Traditionally, the newly wed woman was usually permitted to work at the beginning of her marriage without social disapproval. Work was seen as an escape from boredom in her new role as a wife or homemaker. Work was also accepted for the experience it would provide her later in life. If she ever wanted to return to the job market after her children were grown, she could fall back on previous work experience. However, the newly married woman was cautioned about working too hard as she was expected to maintain the major household responsibilities. Occasionally, couples were warned not to let the wife work, as they may become financially dependent on the two incomes. The couple would then have a difficult financial adjustment when the wife became pregnant and quit her job.

Taboos existed against women working outside the home when the couple had preschool children. Social pressures dictated that younger children needed their mother at home. If the mother did work, the assumption was that she would probably be too fatigued to continue the pace necessary to balance all her duties. After all, she was still expected to handle the major responsibilities for childcare at night, keep up with the household chores, and maintain a job outside the home.

Mothers with school-aged children and older children were given more freedom in the decision to work. When the children were in school all day or grown up and out of the home, the wife's outside job was considered a time-filler or financial supplement to the husband's income.

Historically, as women became more entrenched in the work force away from home, marital priorities began to shift. No longer did the wife view her position as second place. She was transforming her position into a place of equal value with that of her husband. Thus, marriages began to reflect the changes in the male and female roles and expectations.

Changing Roles

Men are discovering that their central dominant position in the relationship has changed. No longer are they the sole economic provider, decision maker, and head of the household. Their sheer physical strength is of less importance, and they are moving toward sharing the traditional female role functions associated with domestic chores and childcare. Men are expected to take part in household chores such as cooking, cleaning, and washing. They encounter new challenges in childcare. Not only are they requested to take part in the logistics of childcare, such as feeding, dressing, and babysitting, but men are also expected to display feelings of patience, understanding, and attachment.

The traditional roles of men have been reshaped in marriage. Men are realizing that contemporary marriages are not like those of their parents. The women they marry no longer fit the role descriptions similar to their own mothers. And their own position is quite different from that of their fathers.

In the past, women were taught that one day they would marry. They were expected to live in their father's house until the big wedding day, at which point, women would then enter a new phase of their lives. But they were still under male control. They were only permitted to leave homes to marry. Women who did not live by these rules often experienced a great deal of negative social pressure. After all, the common view held that women were unable to take care of themselves and needed a provider. Women were encouraged to dream that a Prince Charming would enter their lives and take care of them forever.

In return for a life of care, a woman would help her husband with his dreams and achievements. Her duty was to bear his children and raise and care for them. She was also expected to keep the family together and take care of the daily home maintenance chores. Her feelings and needs were placed second to those of her husband and children. Her wifely duties and toils were rewarded with a comfortable home and the knowledge that she provided the emotional support for her husband and her children. She was essentially serving as the unifying force in the family.

Women are no longer content with traditional, submissive, dependent roles. Women want to take an active part in their lives, rather than sitting back and allowing others to take care of them and make the decisions for them. Women are asserting their own rights of equality in the marriage. They want a partnership based on mutual love, respect, worth, and value.

In traditional marriages, the husband was the economic provider. The family's financial status was solely dependent on the man's income. The wife was only expected to provide emotional support to encourage her husband's success and achievement. If the housewife did work outside the home, her salary was considered extra or supplemental money.

In most families today, the man no longer carries the total financial burden. The family income consists of contributions from both husband and wife. These facts can add up to potential marital conflicts. A husband with traditional views can feel inadequate as a provider. He is no longer a central role. If his salary is not sizable enough to meet the family budget, he can resent his wife's income. The potential also exists for one of the partners to be threatened if the other earns more or as much. A wife's salary can be a catalyst for conflict if each partner fails to respect and admire the other's worth.

In the past, women were expected to choose between marriage and a career. Women were influenced from early ages to consider raising a family as their life career. An additional career outside the home was not advocated. The only females who had their own careers were unfortunate widows who had no money and unmarried spinsters who could not find a husband.

If a woman did have a job prior to marriage or the birth of the first child she knew that she would have to give it up. The possibility did exist, however, that she may return to work later in life, after her family was grown. These ideas are no longer accepted without question. Women are combining marriage with careers.

Relationships within the marriage have had to adjust to the inherent problems with a dual-career couple. No longer are a woman and the entire family expected to adjust completely to certain inevitabilities with a man's job. Marriage partners have begun mutually to agree on promotions or job offers that benefit only one of the careers. Conflicts often occur if one partner is called on to sacrifice a career for the advancement of the other partner. A woman with specialized training may be limited in finding a job in the city where her husband is transferred because of his job. She may find that the life as a suburban housewife is not meeting her needs. The husband, on the other hand, may refuse a promotional transfer for the benefit of his wife's carrer, and as a result negate the chance for further advancement. In this conflict, as well as in the others that will occur in a dual-career marriage, logic and mutual respect can help alleviate stress. Both partners can help reduce conflicts if they understand the other's profession as well as their own professional goals.

Contemporary Marriages

Contemporary marriages are also reflecting new patterns of emerging domestic roles. In the past, women were expected to assume all the housework and childcare responsibility. The management and upkeep of a beautiful home was the wife's duty. Even if she worked outside the home, she was still expected to keep up with the daily chores for the family. The woman was expected to prepare meals, provide clean laundry, and maintain an immaculate house. A working wife who is in a conventional marriage may feel frustration with her double role as a homemaker and career woman. She may resent the fact that she shares her hard earned income with all of the family members, but none of them share in household chores. She may be overwhelmed with the total responsibility to meet the family's everyday needs. Again a woman may experience conflicting feelings about the one-sided nature of her all-encompassing contributions to the family.

The emerging patterns show an equalization in the division of labor of household chores. Both partners are sharing domestic duties. This trend is also displayed in childcare expectations. Childcare duties have begun to shift from female-dominated responsibilities to a joint husband and wife responsibility.

The traditional mothering role which dictated that the female take complete care of the children is being transformed into a parenting role shared by both partners. The total responsibilities of a woman toward children in a marriage are being replaced with shared responsibilities by both parents. Men are beginning to take an active role in the management of child needs.

Conventional marriage patterns are changing as different roles emerge for both the male and female. Couples are marrying later and having fewer children. In more marriages than ever before, both partners are working. Women are achieving higher educational levels and obtaining better jobs, thus placing new demands and role expectations on men, especially concerning home and childcare responsibilities. Contemporary marriages hold many risks. Despite the risk of conflict, couples are still preferring marriage as a way of life.

MAKING THE CHOICE

Women are consciously making decisions to marry or remain single. One woman, Carrie, grew up with many of the conventional expectations concerning marriage. Throughout her life she considered the possibility and consequences of marriage on many occasions. She remembered that she first began to think seriously about marriage on her sixteenth birthday when her parents surprised her with the gift of a large cedar hope chest. Her mother later led her to the attic, where Carrie had often seen a similar chest that had been her mother's. From it, Carrie's mother pulled out her own wedding gown and gave it to Carrie. It was the first treasured item in the new wooden chest.

While Carrie was holding the gown, her thoughts drifted away from reality and toward the future. She imagined her own wedding day. She could visualize walking down the aisle arm in arm with her father and wearing the dress that her mother had given her. She saw a tall, handsome man waiting at the altar. She thought that her life with the man of her dreams would be wonderful. She envisioned the children that would follow . . . a boy and then a girl. The girl would have brown eyes and blonde hair like herself, and the boy would have dark hair and blue eyes like her Prince Charming. She soon realized that several hours had passed and her mother was calling her to dinner.

Carrie began to speculate about her future life. Although she loved, respected, and appreciated her mother, Carrie wasn't sure if she wanted the same type of life for herself. The more Carrie thought about her future as a wife and mother, the closer she came to realize that this way of life may not be her only option. She began to wonder about alternatives other than the traditional expectations of marriage.

In high school, Carrie went to a career counseling workshop. She learned that several fields, especially nontraditional fields, held opportunities for women. She also realized that if she wanted to take advantage of these opportunities she would have to receive further training in the field of her interests.

By graduation, several of her other friends were planning to get married. She had been dating one boy for a year. Everyone told them that they made the perfect couple. Carrie and her boyfriend were even voted Prom Queen and King. All she lacked was the engagement ring. Her boyfriend was willing to become engaged, but Carrie had strong reservations. She remembered the career counselor's advice on college and jobs. She felt she wanted to go to college first, and after her education was completed, she would think about marriage. Her boyfriend did not understand. He had a job waiting in his father's automobile parts store. He felt that he could provide an adequate living for the two of them.

Carrie decided she wanted to attend college and train for a job that could give her new opportunities. She did not want to grow old facing a life of housework. She felt that her future held exciting possibilities. She knew that she was more fortunate than her mother in that she was aware of the choices available to her.

Carrie did enter college and majored in business. She geared her training toward a job in business sales and marketing. The decision to attend college delayed her engagement to her high school sweetheart. Eventually, the romance ended, as Carrie attended a college some distance away.

Carrie pursued her studies and developed a close relationship with a fellow student. Carrie, however, began to feel a rift in the relationship as graduation drew near. In looking for jobs, she hoped they would both find positions in the same city, but this did not occur. Again, she was faced with the decision to marry or remain single. Although she felt that Chad would be able to provide her with a nice life, she knew that she could not be content in a dependent situation. She realized several years before that she needed to pursue her own goals and attain her own successes. Thus, Carrie accepted her best offer, which was miles apart from Chad. Their weekend visits and letters dwindled to once a month, and soon after, the couple saw each other only occasionally. Companionship had been the basis of the relationship and when that was no longer feasible, both Chad and Carrie said good-bye to each other.

Carrie has received several promotions since her college days and she enjoys her marketing job. In the past year, she met Ted, whose career is similar to her own. They support and respect the other's profession and personal goals and accomplishments. Again the topic of marriage surfaces. Carrie feels that marriage would deepen and strengthen the love between them. However, both fear that marriage may bring forth feelings of loss of independence. Ted and Carrie know that the bonds of love between them are very strong. In this case the decision to marry will depend on their needs and feelings of love.

Carrie's experiences taught her that women can take an active part in the determination of their own destiny. Women have the opportunity to view all the alternatives for their future, and have begun to make their own major life choices.

Both men and women are adjusting to new role expectations in single life and in marriages. The emergence of changing roles in both lifestyles brings forth situations that hold potential conflict. Women have begun to take risks for the advancement of their own needs. They have realized that they have the decision to marry or remain single. They have also discovered that whatever choice they make, they face possible conflicts. Women are preparing themselves to meet conflicts, and as a result, are opening up a whole new life.

3

The Decision: Children?

THE DECISION to have children or remain childfree is one of the most difficult decisions facing women today. A lot of thought and energy is expounded by a woman working through such a decision. In many cases, it culminates in an inner struggle of one's value system and priorities. A woman's life situation and the social expectations placed on her further complicate the struggle.

A woman deals with many issues when deciding whether or not to have children. She questions her purpose in life. She examines her existence as a total woman. She has concerns that deal with the social world in which she lives and interacts.

Approaching this complex topic is a difficult matter. A woman begins by identifying the feelings inside herself. She can then relate her feelings to the world around her. It is at this point that she can come to grips with the prospects of making a decision.

TRADITIONAL EXPECTATIONS

The traditional expectation of romance is for young people to meet, fall in love, get married, and of course, raise a family. Young people are indoctrinated with this concept early in life.

Males are encouraged to think about the future in terms of being a provider for a wife and children. The very thought of the word *wife* brings with it the word *children*. Males are encouraged to view children as a necessary family component. How else will the family name be carried on? How else can one achieve the status of "head of the household;" Who will the young boy someday be able to take fishing or to ballgames if he doesn't have children of his own?

Ron, thirty-nine, has been married to his second wife for three years. In his first marriage, which ended in divorce, he did not have any children. He never gave the issue of children much thought until his first marriage ended. "When I divorced I was thirty-three; I realized that if I died suddenly, there would be nothing of me left behind. Since I was an only child, my family name, customs, and heritage would also die. Everything I have worked for in life would be lost. I thought of times past spent with my own dad. I thought of how he must have felt during those times. For the first time in my life I felt a bond with my dad. I longed to have those same experiences with a child of my own. Sometimes I think I remarried just to have children. Maybe I did . . . but I don't regret it."

In some cases, fatherhood is directly associated with masculinity. The reproduction of a child proves to the world a man's sexual capabilities. In this view a boy becomes a man with the birth of his child.

Deep-rooted social values reinforce the concept that all females should want to be mothers. The very thought of remaining childfree cuts against the grain of expected adult female behavior. Females are conditioned to be mothers. Even when very young, girls are geared toward motherhood.

June recalled, "I always knew that when I grew up, I'd have several children. When I was young, my favorite rainy-day game with my sisters was to list as many baby names as possible. We would make a long list of names and would pick our favorite ones. Believe it or not, the names of my children came from those childhood lists."

As children, females are encouraged to play traditional female patterns. Appropriate games are "playing house" and "being a mommy." They are given toys such as dolls and doll carriages. They are given more responsibility with younger siblings in the home. After all, someday they will be performing similar duties and must prepare themselves accordingly.

Holly looked back with some discontent toward her older brothers. She recalls having to stay home and take care of the younger children in the family, while her brothers were able to go out. Her parents would make her babysit, but not her older brothers. She felt that her brothers took advantage of their free time for fun while she had to stay home and be a little mother to her siblings. As young women, females were encouraged to be homemakers.

Girls have occasionally questioned for themselves the value of educational training beyond high school. They have been programmed since childhood to look forward to the day when they could be wives and mothers. Many wonder if the cost and time of a college education are worth the investment.

Mary, a twin and only girl in a family of five children, wanted to go to college. Her parents put her three older brothers through college and were making plans for her twin brother to go. When she asked her father about financial support for school, he told her that he could not afford two children in college at the same time and, said her father, "Your brother has priority because you'll just get married someday anyway. So why should I spend money just for you to find a husband?"

When college pursuits were practical, training in certain fields was encouraged. These fields included teaching, nursing, home economics, and work that could complement the role of wife and mother. These professions would allow the female the time flexibility to work when the children were in school and be home when the children were at home.

Girls have been brought up with the notion that their life should be geared toward motherhood. All else comes second. The concept that womanhood comes with motherhood is developed early and reinforced through adult years. Girls grow up believing that the birth of a child brings out the total woman within.

Robin, forty-eight, first married two years ago. She feels her life has been most rewarding. She is an English professor, has written five books, and is in the process of writing her sixth. As she looked back over the past twenty-five years, she remarked that she spent a great deal of time struggling with her identity as a single female. She struggled with the emotional aspects of womenhood and motherhood issues that were prevalent when she was a young woman. She recalled that her young adult years were permeated with an inner conflict resulting from expectations and values taught to her as a child.

My mother had an underlying assumption of the concept of motherhood and womanhood. She fused the two topics together as one entity. I, on the other hand, have been able to separate the idea of being a woman from being a woman who is also a mother. This has enabled me to establish and accept my own feminine individuality.

EXPECTATIONS IN TRANSITION

The concept that a female can grow up to be a fulfilled and whole woman, independent of motherhood, has emerged and is expanding. Both the positive and negative aspects of motherhood are being examined. Women are becoming aware that they have the choice to have children, but with this awareness comes the pain of decision. The right to make the child versus childfree decision is becoming more accepted. This has not always been true in the past. Family planning was not commonly viewed as a choice. A child "came along" rather than being planned.

Many women who are now older relate their childbearing years to a time in which they felt little control over their lives. The threat of pregnancy hung over them and always seemed to get in the way of future planning. This happened to Jessica. She grew up in a family of three girls. Her husband, Ed, had two brothers and one sister. Jessica and Ed never planned any of their five children. They stated that in post-World War II days, when they first married, husbands and wives had limited choices of birth control methods. They usually relied on rhythmn and sometimes a lot of luck. Jessica noted, "In those days Ed and I didn't discuss pregnancy before it happened. We just discussed pregnancy in relationship to how we would cope with another baby after I was already pregnant."

Issues concerning women and the child versus childfree decision have been expressed for several years. These, however, were not always popular. In the mid-1940s, Helene Deutsch wrote *Psychology of Women* in two volumes. She identified the psychological needs, social pressures, and problems of women at that time. The second volume was entirely devoted to motherhood. She identified motherhood as both the biological process and the psychological experience.[1] In the early 1950s, Simone de Beauvoir wrote *The Second Sex* in which she explored the sexual, social, biological, and historical aspects of women. She stated that a woman has to make independent decisions for her own benefit.[2] In the early 1960s, controversial articles appeared that were against motherhood and emphasized positive aspects of a childfree life.

The early 1970s began an era more tolerant toward the idea of a

---

[1] Helene Deutsch, *The Psychology of Women, Volume II—Motherhood* (New York: Bantam Books, 1973).

[2] Simone de Beauvoir, *The Second Sex*, tr. and ed. H.M. Parshley (New York: Vintage Books, 1974).

childfree life. Permissible social attitudes facilitated a more open acceptance of articles and books that questioned motherhood. Because of the changing social awareness, books that went against the traditional patterns of motherhood received favorable endorsements as well as negative criticisms. At the same time, NON (National Organization for Nonparents) was founded and Planned Parenthood was gaining momentum.

In the mid- to late 1970s, the literature began to reveal a new look at women. The new look advocated women as independent, knowledgable individuals. For the first time, women were encouraged to look at both parenthood and nonparenthood. Reasons to wait for children and deciding factors to have children were being critically and openly discussed. Women were urged to look at both the positive and negative consequences of having children. Attitudinal changes toward the traditional views of having a baby have been reflected in the media and literature over the past decade.

Reasons for the change in attitude toward family planning is in part due to increased knowledge and use of birth control, the availability of medical procedures such as amniocentesis, and the improved safety of abortions. It has only been in the recent decades that reliable birth control methods have been developed. The use of birth control has increased approximately 70 percent by married couples in the last twenty years.[3] The convenience of the pill has made a large contribution to the use of birth control. Permanent birth control operations such as tubular ligation and vasectomy have been made safer and easier and have been accepted as a viable option by couples choosing to limit the size of their families.

The development in the last fifteen years of a more tolerant society has laid the foundation for the acceptance of personal rights, including the right of a woman to choose to have a baby. Changing attitudes toward women, specifically, have increased the awareness of the right to that decision. The increased numbers of females in the working world and the development of professional careers have advanced the need for and acceptability of family planning. Pressure applied from advocates of zero population growth as well as the increase in the cost of living have also contributed to the social acceptance of the child versus childfree decision.

---

[3] Elizabeth M. Whelan, *A Baby . . . Maybe* (New York-Indianapolis: Bobbs-Merrill, 1975), p. 11.

However, individuals involved in this decision still feel a great deal of social pressure as well as inner emotional struggles.

SOCIAL PRESSURES

Although the child versus childfree decision is becoming more acceptable, society still exerts an unwritten but well-established set of rules concerning parenthood. The set of rules comes in the form of social pressure. Children are expected, but not too soon, too late, or too many. Pressures come from many sources. Family members, including parents, in-laws, grandparents, and adult siblings are often the most direct source. Friends, acquaintances, and business associates express their set of expectations. Pressures can also come from religious beliefs and cultural traditions.

Pressure from family members to have children can become very uncomfortable for the childfree couple. Family gatherings, especially during holidays, become a prime opportunity for comments such as "When am I going to get a new grandchild?" or "When is little Susie going to have a cousin to play with?" Often, these questions develop into guilt-producing statements. Other statements that make a couple feel guilty for not obliging are "I'm an old man now, with not too many years left; you're not going to deprive me of a grandchild, are you?" And "I want to see a baby named after me before I die." When couples have decided to delay children for several years, they usually receive subtle and at times direct comments from friends and relatives.

Neil and Renee were totally unprepared when a relative directly questioned the reason behind their delay to have children. Neil, twenty-four, and Renee, twenty-three, had been married for four years. They both were college graduates and Renee had completed graduate work in education. She was a teacher and Neil owned a small retail operation. Their professional careers were just beginning, and they felt their careers needed to develop before they had children. At a family gathering, Renee's father asked Neil to sit down for a talk. He questioned Neil in a serious manner about the sexual relationship of the two. The father-in-law assumed that absence of sex was the reason for the couple's childlessness.

Another incident involved a woman in her late twenties who had been married for eight years. Her distraught grandmother told her that she was praying for her every night so that she would not be barren the rest of her life.

Some women in their early thirties have commented on the feeling they have that "time is running out." They have been met with numerous statements from well-meaning friends and relatives. Emily, who is thirty-two, had been married to Jack for nine years, and they had no children. Emily was a homemaker who used her time for pottery and crafts. She enjoyed staying home and did not feel the financial need to work since Jack's income was sufficient to maintain their desired lifestyle. Both were comfortable with their situation and felt they had a happy life together. Emily, however, was completely astounded when her older sister questioned her about children. The sister informed Emily that "her time was running out and unless she got pregnant soon she might as well forget it."

Pressure from a sister or brother is difficult to handle. Glenda, in her late thirties, had been married for six years. Her older sister, Maureen, stated that she was breaking a family tradition. Explained Maureen, "Thanksgiving and Christmas wouldn't be any fun if each member didn't have any children! After all," she said, "What are holidays for?" She further told Glenda that other family members were "very concerned" about the situation.

Childfree couples who move into their first house, or into a larger house, are often reminded of their childfree state. Relatives and friends make comments such as "now that you have more room you can plan a child." A favorite comment is "this bedroom will make a perfect nursery," or "this backyard is ideal for a sandbox and swingset."

Gary and Abby had been married for three years. When they bought their first home, he was twenty-four and she was twenty-three. They met in high school and married soon after graduation. Abby worked as a secretary and Gary worked for his father at a family-owned furniture business. Gary's father decided to help them with the down payment for their home. Before they ever moved into the house, pressure to start a family began. Gary's father announced that his loan to them would be "paid off" when they had a child. The down payment loan seemed to be an investment for grandchildren.

When either an adult sibling or a friend has a baby, comments usually follow. One such remark is "now it's your turn." If the childfree woman happens to hold a newborn she may be asked if she wants to hold one of her very own. Friends may also comment about how natural she is with a baby or that she must be practicing for her time to come.

The parents of a childfree woman can apply pressure when they relate the "grandchildren" stories of their friends. One mother expressed her feelings on the topic in a guilt-producing manner. She told her thirty-four-year old daughter that she became depressed because she always had to look at pictures of other people's grandchildren and didn't have a picture of her own to show.

Women are frequently asked at social gatherings whether or not they have children. A negative response often terminates the conversation or evokes an inquisitive statement. The childfree woman may find herself in a position of either explaining or defending the fact that she has no children. The reverse is rarely seen: The individual who has children is seldom requested to explain her reasons for having them.

Claudia, thirty-nine, is married and has a career. She and her husband, Dan, have no children. An incident occurred at a dinner party with Dan's co-workers and their spouses. Dan is in a male-dominated field, and consequently, most of the spouses were wives. Claudia was trying to make conversation with a few of the wives when one of them turned to her and said, "How many children do you have?" Claudia answered that she had no children. Before she could give further comment, another woman asked, "What do you do?" Claudia started to describe her career. Another woman at the table interrupted her by stating, "Oh, you don't have any! You must have a lot of free time."

Religious doctrine can influence the decision to have children. Practicing members of the Catholic faith, for example, believe that birth control is against church doctrine. Thus, the decision to have children is not a personal decision but rather adheres to religious tradition. Practicing members of the Mormon church advocate large families, so the decision to have children is assumed to be an acceptable one.

Marge was forty-three when she became pregnant with her sixth child. Her religious beliefs did not permit birth control or termination of pregnancy. She described the social disapproval she experienced when she said, "I've tried to follow my conscience. People may complain if you don't have children, but if you have too many that's even worse! I love all my children and wouldn't trade any of them for all the social acceptance or riches in the world; but if I had to do it all over again, I would do it differently."

The unwritten social rules of parenthood exert expectations on individuals with children as well as on those without. The unmarried pregnant female does not rate the same degree of acceptance or understanding as a married pregnant female. Women who are over thirty-five, sometimes feel negative social reactions to a pregnancy. Families with two, three, or four children can feel pressure by the advocates of zero population growth.

Society places a heavy burden of guilt on the female who does not want children. She wonders "What's wrong with me?" and "Why am I so different from my friends?" Some childfree women feel stigmatized by others who may see her as materialistic, selfish, irresponsible, and self-centered.

The female who is aware of her own feelings can come to grips with negative social pressures. Many times, both partners in the relationship share in the decision. Both individuals should be aware of the pressures and realize that the decision to have children or remain childfree is a very personal one and can be very complex.

The child versus childfree decision is basically an emotional one. Although practical issues exert influence on the decision, these issues do not provide the underlying force. The foundation for the decision comes from feelings and emotions. Feelings are the expression of the underlying emotional makeup and are often confused, complex, and at times masked.

Feelings can reflect the personal and social values of an individual's circumstances. If a woman can break through the social value system and identify her own inner feelings, she can begin to understand the complex set of issues involved in this decision.

The decision to have or not have a child is a major life decision. Both sides of the decision should be thoroughly examined. The choices carry irrevocable implications with pluses and minuses. The decision to have a child is a permanent one. A child cannot be returned or exchanged. The child brings vast responsibilities and commitment that last a lifetime. The decision to remain childfree also has finality. When the decision results in sterilization, the process is usually irrevocable. Neither decision has a set of guarantees for future happiness. The individual doesn't know if she will experience a change in her life priorities or attitudes. The importance of the child or childfree decision was summarized by Whelan in *A Baby? . . . Maybe* when she stated that "the decision to have a child is the most fateful lifetime decision that will directly affect an entire future. What's at stake, after all is just the rest of your life and maybe some unborn person's life too."[4]

[4]*Ibid.*, p. 198.

Identification of the issues and inner feelings concerning the child versus childfree decision is difficult. One may begin by looking at both sides of the issue.

CHILDREN: YES

The decision to have children can generate feelings of joy, fear, and excitement. The very thought of having a baby can evoke a new hope for the future. For some women the birth of a child represents a private victory over mortality. Other women decide to have children because they simply love children and want a child of their own. Some women, on the other hand, are overwhelmed with the responsibility for the care of a new life. Feelings about this decision, and reasons for having children, are as individual and numerous as the women making the decision.

Children have been born because the individual involved has chosen to avoid making a decision. Many accidental pregnancies have occurred this way. Some women have realized that they never thought about the choice available until after it was too late. These women never examined the advantages and disadvantages of life with children. They never gave the decision consideration before pregnancy.

Social pressure or conformity can be a motivating factor behind the decision to have a child. Many women, after a few years of marriage, find themselves being asked when they are going to have children. They are questioned about why they are childfree. Many do not realize they have the option to challenge societal role expectations. They, like their inquirers, assume pregnancy to be a natural part of marriage and womanhood.

Leslie, thirty-two, is a model and artist. She and her husband, Charles, have discussed the possibility of children but have delayed making a decision. As of late, both sets of in-laws have been applying an enormous amount of pressure on Leslie so that she will have a child. Leslie's father went to his bank and inquired about setting up a trust fund for future grandchildren. Charles has no strong feelings about having children, but Leslie feels that at this point in her career she does not want to take the time to have a child even though pressure from her family continues.

The birth of a child can be the expression of love shared by two people evolving as a natural part of marriage. Feelings of love can be the major factor in the decision to have a child. The baby becomes a symbol. It is viewed as an extension of love and it can enrich and strengthen the bond between the couple. Laurie and John are an example of two people having children because they desire to share the love between them. Laurie is twenty-nine and John is thirty-two. They both have separate professional careers. For the past two years they have been discussing the issue and have made the joint decision to extend and share their love with a baby. They feel that a baby will be an added blessing to their marriage.

Happy childhood memories can be a positive reinforcement in the decision to have children. Some women wish to relive their own childhood experiences by having children. They want to model their own mothers.

Others view the decision to have a child as a way to live missed experiences. This sentiment is expressed by statements such as "I want to give my children the good parts of life I never had" or "I want their life to be better than mine was."

Some women are motivated by the desire to relive or change their own past experiences. They want to prove they are different from their own mothers. Thus, their experiences serve as a strong motivation but in a different direction. They are seeking to prove something to themselves, and in so doing, they are making a statement to others.

There are both positive and negative reasons why women choose to have children. Social pressures, goal fulfillment, desire to leave a living legacy, love, avoidance of loneliness, proof of womanhood, and the desire to experience pregnancy itself are among the most common reasons. The desire to be a mother has also been traced to a natural instinct. Traditional psychoanalysts such as Freud and Erickson equated the wish to have a baby with an instinctive quality innate to women. Freud believed motherhood to be basic to the well-adjusted female. Erikson felt that the major life role for a woman was to reproduce. Deutsch was of the opinion that the emotional relationship between mother and child is so deep and primitive that it transcends all social and individual differences.[5]

Women choose to have children for many reasons, but once the decision is made, it is final. Some women are surprised by the unexpected joys of motherhood, and they alter their career plans to follow the emotions of maternity. A thirty-one-year-old graduate of an Eastern university had been a social worker until she had a baby. Her husband was training to finish his medical degree, so she went back to work part time to help out with expenses. When he graduated and received a position, she chose to stay home until their child was in school. It was simply the choice she

[5]Deutsch, p. 5.

wanted to make. Now the child is her priority and she has no intention of returning to work.

There are some narcissistic elements in the decision to have children. First, a child is an extension of the self—an egocentric focus. Loving a child is closely tied with loving oneself. When one sees qualities in children which are undesirable, one is quick to blame those qualities on someone else—like spouse, Uncle Harry or mother-in-law Sue.

Secondly, having a child is a demonstration of autonomy, achievement, and power. The act says, "Look what I did". The power lies in the total control over another human being—the power to teach, to manipulate, to love or to withdraw that love. Women possess great power as the guardians of children. They can mold personalities, infuse attitudes and prejudices, and influence development. Children are immensely vulnerable to a mother's mood and feelings. Many women have traded this job as mother for a "successful" career. In the public world, they are carrying out a submissive role. They yielded to motherhood. In the private world, a mother is the queen—the final authority and the expert on the home front. The emotional stability of mothers weighs heavily upon the impact they have on children.

Some women equate the birth of a child with becoming an adult. A female in her twenties stated that upon the birth of her first child, she felt accepted into the adult world. She finally felt an equal status with her own parents. She felt that she had finally been initiated. She had proven her womanhood.

A few women have expressed the hope of saving a marriage with a pregnancy. Some women feel that a child can bring a positive change to a somewhat dull marriage. They fail to understand the strains that pregnancy and child-rearing can add to an already weak relationship.

Pregnancy can also be used as an excuse for quitting an unfulfilling or overly demanding job. A child can provide a legitimate reason to leave a job. For a woman who is bored with her position or "tired of working," motherhood presents a tantalizing escape from the doldrums of the working world. Without a child, a woman may feel that she has no valid excuse for resigning.

There are numerous reasons to have a child. A child brings both positive and negative consequences. Individuals who have decided to have children can add wonderful enrichment to their lives. The positive experience with children can be maximized for those who are fully aware of the possible consequences of life with children.

Consequences of Life
with Children

Bringing up a child can be a challenging endeavor which can enhance and brighten every aspect of life. The decision to meet the challenge deserves much consideration. Factors to be weighed in this decision range from the emotional effects the child has on the life of a woman to the sobering reality of the awesome responsibilities involved when raising a child.

The presence of children in a marriage can help formulate a strong unity between a man and a woman. The experiences associated with children can provide opportunities for bonding in the lives of a couple. Two people can learn and grow together while their child is learning and growing.

Children can also cause severe strains on a relationship. Feelings of isolation and jealousy can arise. The time and energy necessary for child-rearing, especially in the first year of life, is physically and emotionally demanding. By the end of a long day a woman can find herself too tired or too exhausted to interact emotionally or sexually with her husband. Without prior understanding of the high demands of motherhood, emotional rifts between spouses can result. Women may find that their once planned and structured life is suddenly altered.

Children do not always meet the expectations of their parents or follow the paths which their parents have planned for them. In other words, they do not always follow in their parents' footsteps. A parent who envisions a child taking over the business may be disappointed when the child shows a lack of interest in assuming the "assigned" responsibilities.

When Peggy and Jim's little boy was born twenty-one years ago, they thought it was the greatest day of their lives. From the beginning they began saving for his education and his legal training in hopes that he would follow in his father's footsteps and become a lawyer. When Jim Jr. was in his junior year of college, he decided that he wanted to pursue a career in engineering rather than in law. His parents were disappointed because they could not totally understand his interest in a different field; they took personally his rejection of law. They never quite understood his career choice.

Children can unexpectedly interfere with previous life priorities. Women who quit their jobs can feel at times as if their career had been sacrificed. A sacrificed career can lead to unresolved emotional conflicts. A woman can have feelings of isolation and think the rest of the world is leaving her behind. She is no longer going out into the world of business. She is no longer having the professional and personal interactions with others that she previously took for granted. She may feel her opportunities for challenge and mental stimulation have been limited or completely cut off.

Before the birth of her child, Jenny was an intern in pediatrics at the university hospital. Her job was very demanding. Although her job had pressure at times, the other staff members helped to create a pleasant atmosphere. Since she has been at home with her twin babies, she has realized that she misses her former co-workers very much. She missed sharing her daily life tales as much as listening to theirs.

She decided she would be happier with some combination of both worlds. She found a private office position where she could work part time a few days a week while her husband worked in research at the university.

When a woman chooses children over an established career, she can experience a loss of identity. She no longer has her job or title to give her personal satisfaction or social acceptance. She finds that she is on her own; unless she has a strong sense of security and self-awareness, she can have a feeling of not belonging. She can think that she's a person without a function or contribution to make to society. She can develop resentment in reaction to either the loss of or absence of her past career. She never before realized how much security the title "Manager of Public Relations" gave her.

A woman may find herself making excuses for being at home or saying, "I used to be. . . ." Women should not apologize for their decision to have children, regardless of the consequences, if it is the decision they have freely chosen with knowledge of the outcome. There is no set of labels which automatically comes with being a homemaker. The feelings many women experience are purely emotional ones, often without justifiable cause. Understanding those feelings can help in their resolution.

Many women find the task of reentering the job market, even after a short break, very difficult. They find that their position has been given to someone else permanently. Very seldom can a woman start back to work at the same level. Many women hear comments such as: "Since you've been out of the field for two years, a lot has happened. It will take you a year or two just to catch up." The implication is that the "new" worker is stale in her former skills. "Why don't you go back to school for a refresher course before you apply for the position?"

It only takes a few comments like these to make a woman feel as if she is out of date. She can feel as if she has been "put away" or "on the shelf" for the past few years. She feels her talents have been placed on "hold".

The consequences of the choice to have children can at times put road blocks in front of an advancing career. The woman who is aware of these consequences can prepare herself for the emotional and practical struggles that follow. A thorough knowledge and understanding of the possible consequences of children on a career can help reduce the risk of damage to a developing or ongoing career.

Children can provide a rich source of joy and contentment. The addition of children to a family unit can add fulfillment and enrichment. A woman expressed her joy of her children when she said, "I can't imagine my life without children. It was a joy to watch each one grow to be an adult and to know I had part in it. My children have added real meaning to my life."

Considerations of the subsequent effects of children can be helpful in the decision to have children. A determination to have a child based on the considerations of both sides of the issue can cultivate a better understanding and acceptance of the child by eliminating the unexpected surprises and frustrations which accompany parenting.

MORE CHILDREN?

The decision to have more children can be as emotionally difficult as the original choice to have the first child. A second, third, or fourth child can complicate an established way of life. A developing career can suffer because of the interruption. Additional responsibilities and demands of childcare can create stress in a marriage. Parents undergo a laborious task when they deal with the issue of more children.

There are many considerations to weigh in this complex decision. Routines will be altered with another child in the family. The effect of this change is a crucial issue. Many women ask themselves if their daily schedule will be manageable. At times, the logistics of the coordination of work, day care, meal preparation, household chores, and childcare can be all too consuming even with one or two children, and the integration of the needs of a second or third child into an already overbooked schedule complicates the issue.

Changes in Relationships

Many women are concerned with the relationship changes that would inevitably occur with additional children. Questions such as these are commonly raised: "Will the other children in the family be upset? Will they feel neglected? How will I be able to spread my time for all the children, my husband, and still have some time left for me? Will my marriage suffer? Are we ready for another child?" Practical issues to bear in mind are the parents' ages and the family budget. Women have experienced apprehensive feelings because of medical reasons. They also felt that they wanted to spend their mid-forties and fifties in ways other than raising teenagers. Financial issues are a substantial factor in making the decision to enlarge the size of the family. "Will I be able to support another child through the college years? What happens if Susie needs glasses at the same time that Johnny needs braces for his teeth? Can we afford the additional food, medical, and clothing expenses of more children?" These are all questions that women have asked themselves prior to making a decision to have more children.

The cost of another child can be too much for a family's income to bear. Many families need both the husband's and the wife's paycheck to survive financially. If the wife drops out of the work force for a year or so, so does her paycheck. In essence, a significant amount of money that helped pay family expenses no longer exists. At the same time, the expenses increase because of the new baby's medical care and ongoing needs, such as diapers, clothes, and baby food. Passed-along clothes are usually threadbare by the third or fourth child. Many families simply cannot afford another child in the family.

Another very real concern is the social pressure which now seems to accompany a large family. Women have remarked that childfree friends, especially successful ones, do not understand why anyone would want more children. Parents who have two children, one boy and one girl, are prone to criticism from their friends and family. If a family has one child of each sex, it supposedly has the perfect balance. Friends are often quite unsympathetic to a couple's desire to have another child, accusing them of overpopulating the world.

Many people do not understand the changes that accompany a life with more children. Arranging babysitters and schedules can become more hectic. At times parents may not want to go out and leave their children with a babysitter, especially if a child is not feeling well or if the parents had to spend a great deal of time away from home because of other commitments. Friends often do not understand, and distances in relationships can develop.

Career Consequences

The decision to have an additional child can be disastrous to a woman's career. If she decides to leave work for a year or two, she may be unable to acquire the same status when she tries to return. She may even have a great deal of difficulty finding a job when she does want to start back to work. Women who do not keep up with their career when they drop out to have children may find themselves passed up by others who never left the job market. Promising careers can be sidetracked. When a woman does reenter, she usually has to work twice as hard to catch up and prove that she still possesses the capabilities and skills to do the job.

The decision to have another child has far-reaching ramifications. All members of the family are affected. The decision itself, is also affected by concerns of finances, relationships, life styles, and social pressures. The decision is not easy; it is very complex and difficult.

Robin and Van have been struggling with this dilemma for several months. Robin is thirty-two and Van is thirty-six. They already have two children, Bobby, two, and Melissa, four. Van is an economic advisor for the state government, and Robin is a psychologist at a child-development center. They both work and are career oriented. Van definitely wants another child. Robin, however, is emotionally dealing with many of the issues confronting women who try to make this decision. Robin wants to have another baby but is afraid of future career consequences and the possible effect on family relations. When asked why she wanted more children, Robin replied, "I grew up in a large family. I loved it. I loved the noise and excitement. And, I really liked being pregnant—it was wonderful. Also, I enjoy my kids. They are so much fun that I think another child will add to the family togetherness. Our family shares so much goodness that I think another child will enhance and expand our happiness." When asked why she was hesitant to have another child, Robin expressed frustration, worry and apprehension.

I don't know if I have the time for another child. I can't accomplish now what I want to; another child would rearrange my schedule. Right now, I have a balanced system for myself worked out. I work part time and I have two days to spend with Bobby and Melissa. I can take them to the park and play with them like a mother should. In this way, I don't have quite as much guilt about working. If I had another baby I would probably have to quit work. I don't want to do that because my career is very important to me. I know I'm not as successful as I could be, but I've chosen to have my two children. If I had a third child, I'm afraid that my career would become very low on the priority list. I'm really scared that will happen. I need to have the adult and professional contact that my career yields. I feel that I have a lot of potential and I really like my work. I seem to be in a constant emotional battle with the idea that I may have to give up my career potential in exchange for another child. I really try to keep a balance for myself among my two children, husband, and career. I do so much to keep my crazy schedule going, I just cannot even imagine thinking about another child.

Many couples have more children simply because they want a larger family. The arrival of an addition to the family creates an opportunity for love to grow and be shared. An additional child can complicate daily schedules. Family priorities can be reorganized. Conflicts often occur in interfamily relationships, finances, leisure time, and professional careers. A woman may be faced with a decision to quit her job or work part time. She may realize that without constant monitoring of both of her worlds, the balance between home and office may be difficult to maintain. The woman who makes the decision whether to have more children will be more satisfied with her choice only after careful evaluation and understanding of the consequences.

CHILDREN: NO

In 1977, the Zero Population Growth Organization reported that 5 percent of the population had declared intentions to remain childfree.[6] The childfree decision is a viable option for a contemporary woman. Improved birth control methods, social attitudinal changes, and the women's rights movement have contributed to make this option a reality.

Embodied in the choice to remain childfree is a very personal and emotionally demanding decision. The traditional assumption that all women should be mothers is no longer accepted without question. Women are critically looking at all the aspects of life without children. Reasons

[6]Boston Women's Health Book Collective, *Ourselves and Our Children* (New York: Random House, 1978), p. 17.

that lead to the childfree decision are numerous in quantity and diverse in nature. The reasons to opt for a childfree life range from a new look at the concept of motherhood to a consideration of the practical aspects of having and raising children.

The underlying motivation for motherhood is in question. In the past, motherhood was viewed as a natural instinct. The opinion that motherhood is directly linked to female instinct is being challenged and criticized. Today, many psychiatrists and sociologists are concurring with the idea that the desire for motherhood is not the result of a natural instinct for reproduction.

Several recent authors have begun to reject the idea that motherhood is linked to a biological instinctive destiny. Jean Baker Miller advocated a new look at traditional women's strengths in *Toward a New Psychology for Women*. She encouraged women to recognize their position and take a new perspective on the topic of the traditional vulnerability and helplessness of instinctive impulses.[7]

Although controversy still exists, instinct is no longer presumed to be the undisputed fundamental cause for the desire of motherhood. Rather, the desire for a child or childfree life is perceived to evolve from a woman's interaction with her total life situation. The sum of the total experience of a woman has a powerful influence on her decision to remain childfree.

Previous experiences can strongly influence decisions made later in life. A woman in her early thirties recalled that her childhood directly influenced her decision to remain childfree. She grew up in an economically strained large family. She witnessed the many sacrifices required of her parents. Extra money was always needed for clothes or doctor bills for the children. She was unable to make similar sacrifices in her adult life, and she decided early that she would not pattern her life after her parents. She saw and interpreted what children had done to their lives and was determined not to repeat those injuries. She will not have children.

Another woman, who was an only child, had been told by her parents at an early age that she was an "accident." She grew up feeling unwanted. Consequently she developed an orientation toward life that did not make children a priority.

A forty-two-year-old married attorney stated that personal freedom

---

[7] Jean Baker Miller, *Toward a New Psychology of Women* (Boston: Beacon Press, 1977).

was her reason for not having a child. She felt in control of her life. She had been able to make a decision that freed her to pursue her major goals.

Conflict: The Trade Off

Many women have expressed the attainment of personal goals as the motivating factor behind their childfree decision. They feel in control of their own lives; able to pursue their own destiny. Many women realize achievement of personal goals through a career. One woman, although she was not involved in a professional career, felt that her life was very active and productive. She valued her freedom to travel and to do what she wanted when she wanted.

Women can experience conflict with the thought of trading off a career for raising a family. Many women in careers have spent years in training. They have already sacrificed a great deal of energy to gain their position. Many women find themselves unwilling to change from their professional role to a maternal role. Others who have delayed the decision many times have realized that numerous postponements can lead to a permanent childfree decision. One woman stated that she had originally planned to have children, but she was so heavily commited to her job that she could no longer see children in her future.

A thirty-eight-year-old television producer stated that she had delayed having a child several times because her career opportunities were too inviting to turn down and her job became too demanding. She felt the time had never been exactly right for her to "slow down" even temporarily. "My career depends on my willingness to work long hard hours. I never know what my schedule will be. Sometimes it is normal for a while and it may suddenly be unbelievable for several weeks or months. I just couldn't depend on my professional energies to carry me through a pregnancy or new motherhood." She was not willing to give up her career or risk slowing down its progression. The full-time career climb with its inherent demands and necessary flexibility in her field was incompatible with motherhood. It was not a realistic option for her.

The fear of losing or changing an established lifestyle can be a determining factor in the childfree decision. By the time many people reach their mid-thirties, they have become accustomed to a childfree life. They are less willing to sacrifice the freedom they have learned to enjoy for a set of restrictions brought about through parenthood.

A child can have a dramatic effect on the lifestyle of the two parents. New financial burdens can alter their once-established financial security.

Freedom of mobility usually comes to a halt. Planning becomes a necessary way of life. Professional, social, and leisure activities once taken for granted can now create severe conflicts with the new responsibilities of caring for a child.

The loss or shift in self-identity is another major reason why some women choose to remain childfree. A thirty-six-year-old corporate executive summed up this perspective by stating, "I used to think about having a baby, but I feared that if I took such a step, I'd be totally consumed in a traditional role. I don't want to jeopardize my self-reliance and independence that I've worked so hard to attain."

An evaluation of the marital relationship can lead to the childfree decision. The addition of children can unbalance an unsteady relationship. This usually occurs when one of the partners is neither ready nor willing to accept a child into his or her life.

Mona, age thirty-three, got married when she was very young. She finished her education and went to work as a loan officer in a bank. Her husband also finished his formal training and expected a promising business career. After five years of marriage, when Mona was twenty-four years old, she began discussing with her husband the possibility of having children. He stated that he had never wanted children because of the economic burden. Although their marriage was weak Mona was unable to accept the reality of the situation. When she was twenty-five she had a tubular ligation at the request of her husband. She had convinced herself that the reason she did not want children was because children would interfere with her career. A few years later her marriage ended. She discovered that the real reason behind her decision was that she did not want children with her first husband. This realization of the true reason for the decision helped her to get a grasp of her feelings although it was too late to change her situation.

The climbing divorce rate has contributed to second thoughts concerning the prospect of children. Divorced women with children often present a discouraging profile to the childfree woman. Raising children alone can result in a very difficult emotional, as well as financial, struggle.

In some cases, practical issues can result in a childfree decision. Some of the more common practical considerations are hereditary and genetic diseases (such as Tay Sachs and sickle cell anemia), age risk (especially after the late thirties), health status of the female, difficulty with current available birth control methods, and lack of financial means to provide for a child.

The decision to remain childfree can develop from a strong belief to limit the world population. This view is advocated by environmentally oriented associations such as the National Organization for Non-Parents and the Zero Population Growth Organization.

Consequences of a Childfree Life

The life of a woman can be fulfilling and rewarding regardless of her decision to have or not have children. The decision to remain childfree carries both positive and negative consequences.

There are many positive effects of a childfree decision. Freedom of lifestyle and feelings of independence are among the positive consequences. Career goals may be easier to achieve. Women who have chosen a childfree life do not have to deal with the guilt of leaving their child in a day-care center or with a babysitter. These women can live their lives as they plan, without regard for the responsibilities of a child.

The negative aspects of a childfree life usually begin with feelings associated with regret. A woman can feel a loss or a deprivation of life's most precious treasures. She may doubt herself as a woman by wondering if she was capable of producing a baby. Social pressure can, at times, be too much to bear. Feelings of future loneliness can be overpowering. She may wonder about her companionship when she is older. She may compare her own future to that of her grandmother and wonder what life without a legacy will be like. A woman may be fearful that at some point she will regret her decision not to have children. She may find herself tormented by questions such as "What if I had a child?" or "I wonder what a child of mine would look like?"

Regardless of the decision, a woman can better understand herself if she investigates the reasons behind her decision and come to grips with her own needs for fulfillment.

Today women are in a position to choose a childfree life or a life with children. The choice for the decision itself can allow the individual woman the freedom to become a fulfilled and total person.

III
FAMILY

4

The Decision: Having Children

ONCE THE DECISION to have a baby has been made, without warning the mind begins to wander seemingly without aim from the world of adulthood into the unknown world of children. The combined fear and excitement of new parenthood may throw lives off their usual steady course. Suddenly, concentration becomes difficult and involvements in the outside world are easily diverted. Focus of life changes from broad interests to narrow fascinations. The changing sphere inside the woman's body demands new attention and it is a natural egocentric interest.

Traditionally, men were never included in this area of women's lives. The total adjustment as well as the decision itself was left up to women. The women's movement and the assertiveness of contemporary females have provided a place for men in the broad spectrum of parenthood beyond the actual conception. Women have finally realized that men want to share in the pregnancy experience. Men and women desire to share in the active process of parenting from the beginning of the child's development in the uterus. The experience presents a time of transition in the roles of both men and women. The total family structure can benefit from such transition. A child now born into the world is expected to have the equal benefits of mother and father. Though in many situations women are still the primary caretakers, the idea of co-parenting is growing steadily out of the increased desire to share the parenting experience.

Having a child is an intense experience. There is no other period of life when we are required to assume such responsibility, such hard work, and such isolation. The decision to have children is unlike any other major life decision in that it is irrevocable and lifelong. The role of parents carries tremendous responsibility, but with it comes the potential for personal fulfillment through the growth and development of another human being. The opportunities for personal involvement are unlike any other experience.

TIMING:
NOW OR LATER?

Timing is obviously a choice in the contemporary world of contraceptive sophistication. Barring the "accidental" pregnancy, many women find it too bold a step to discontinue contraception. Sometimes it is not the idea of a baby that is being postponed, but the decision of when to become pregnant.

Quite a number of women wait until the perfect time to have that baby, but the perfect time never arrives. The perfect time is the period of life in which all the desired conditions for parenthood have been met. Some women may rush through their twenties postponing the decision about childbearing and motherhood. They may have postponed the decision about the right man or the right time in a career or the security of a set of financial conditions. Still they carry childhood fantasies and expectations of motherhood.

There is no perfect time for parenting. For some women, one period of life may have certain advantages over another. For other women, it does not matter. Postponement brings with it no guarantees of less conflict or complications. The parenthood experiences may be somewhat altered but the quality of those experiences cannot be predicted for anyone.

The irony is that this decision many times rests on career and money. Couples wait to have a child until they can afford it. So the wife drops out of the work force; the couple is down to a single paycheck; their expenses are increasing; and they have already outgrown the home they could afford. Although it is true that women are remaining childfree longer than ever before, statistics still show that most women expect to have children. Many women, even career women, hold to childhood memories and the traditional expectations established for them as girls growing up.

Because of changing conditions, postponement of motherhood is a viable choice. Delayed parenting is not only socially accepted but also often advocated. Many reasons are implied socially and economically as well. Couples are expected to be financially stable in their living conditions and bank account; psychologically, in their level of maturity; and emotionally, in their self-esteem and relationship. Many couples feel direct pressure to achieve all these goals in order to meet the "perfect condition" which signals a green light to go ahead and have a baby.

Medical advances have supported the choice to postpone parenthood. In addition to the ability to control fertility, other medical advances such as anmiocentesis have revised the outer limit of safe childbearing. Women now have a longer period of postponement or more time in which to make up their minds. Some women in their mid- to late thirties may completely change their ideas of their twenties or they may have a restlessness which they feel motherhood might cure. There is also the thought that "time is running out." A woman may look back and wish she had borne a child years earlier for the companionship she may seek in looking ahead.

There are many reasons to postpone having a child. Some women just do not find the right partner or do not have the financial security they think they need. Some may not have the motivation they desire before entering motherhood. Postponement of motherhood until the late twenties or early thirties is a trend among college-educated women. They may not postpone children temporarily but do so for as long as it takes to prepare themselves personally, maritally, and professionally. Psychological readiness is a critical ingredient in deciding to have children. Some women need the freedom of the twenties, the time to explore, experiment, advance, plan, and clarify.

Lives of women are more complex now than they have been in the past. There is more happening. Thus, "dropping out" for nine months or a few years may seem like too much of a sacrifice. Ambition, too, is a concept women can openly admit instead of hiding it in a closet or seeking it vicariously through a husband. Delay of parenthood provides time to launch a career and become well established to assure against loss of that career. The desire to succeed in a career is a critical factor in the conflict surrounding the decision to have a child.

More women now feel that parenting is a joint effort, and they are willing to say so publicly and stick with their opinion. They enter into the agreement of parenthood on that basis, and most of these women have tested the strength of the emotional bonds in their marriage before coming to a final decision. These young couples have learned collaboration in household routines and know how to transfer that partnership in the processes of parenting. Though few couples split parenting chores fifty-fifty (and this would be extremely difficult to do continuously), they are prepared to implement flexibility when needed.

The timing of the decision to have a child is also affected by the importance of the strength of a relationship. Both women and men place greater emphasis than ever before on the quality of a relationship. The high rate of divorce indicates that people do not stay in an unsatisfactory marriage, as was customary in the past. Many couples want to "make sure" their relationship is solid before creating a symbol of their life together. The stress and strains of having a child will never serve to solidify a shaky relationship. A couple must have intimacy, humor, and love in order to weather the storms of the parenting adventure. Time is sometimes needed to determine if parenthood is really desirable or if one or both partners are mature enough to enter into such a venture.

For other couples, biological infertility makes having a child a decision of adoption. If the desire to become a parent is present, through the efforts of counseling and adoption a couple's wishes can be fulfilled. However once the decision is made, there can be a delay of two to five years or even longer before they can receive a child. The rigorous routines of interviews, form after form to complete, and analysis of marriage and lifestyle are often more than some couples want to bear.

Those couples, not knowing about problems of fertility, who have postponed the decision to become parents are faced with an entirely new perspective. Some couples wonder that if they had decided to have children earlier in life they may have been able to bear children. This can be emotionally difficult.

Timing and a Career

Couples also time having babies for career reasons. Men seldom think about this because they are traditionally insulated from the daily routines of parenthood and thus are only indirectly affected on an immediate time scale. It is mainly women who are caught in the dilemma of family and career, and thus it is the woman's time that must be interrupted. In regard to the career advantages of postponing children, there is an unencumbered period of time to earn a degree, ripen a talent, develop a set of skills, and use those talents in satisfying work. These are natural and expected career goals for men, but for women to reach this level takes deliberate planning and careful monitoring of career goals. Women who have followed this pattern feel that their professional lives would never have developed if they had stopped to have children in younger years.

Women who want to take an active part in the care of their children and who have also carved out careers for themselves may find it beneficial to postpone parenthood until they begin to envision a "career lull" for the first year or two of parenthood. Of course, no one can ever be certain that career commitments will remain as predicted. Occasionally, a career may coincidentally ripen with the peaking of family responsibilities. A woman in her thirties or forties with young children may experience conflicts between demands of the children and new or additional professional demands growing out of her established career. She may have a need to travel more often, attend conferences and meetings, and be called away when she prefers to be at home. This may be more difficult for the woman who carefully planned motherhood, as her well-made plans go astray and her aspirations and expectations for motherhood are shattered. Even though they are typically strong women, it is a double demand to extend their capabilities and their coping energies.

Many women decide to time having a baby with their career schedule. An actress, writer, teacher, or designer can decide more easily than women in some other careers when she wants to have a baby conveniently. Since the needs of children differ according to their stage of development, the demands on the mother will vary. This is universally accepted to be true by most specialists in the field of child development or child psychology. The mother has traditionally been the primary caretaker, and the needs of the child will affect her in terms of demands on her time and scheduling of her own activities. Sometimes working even part time can fit in well with one stage of development and conflict with another. Generally, however, this depends on the child and how the parents structure the situation. If a mother's absence does not threaten the child's security, usually there will be no effect on him or her.

Sandy, an actress, realized later than most women that she did have a choice between working and not working. She had started acting as an adolescent, and since her parents encouraged her, she never thought about not working. At times, she recalled, she was the breadwinner for her family. Sandy began to have feelings similar to those of women who had never worked. She felt a narrow direction in her life and wondered about exploring possible options. She realized there were other ways to live her life besides the way in which she was programmed as a child.

I remember thinking as a child that once you got married, you automatically gave up your career. I thought you couldn't work and be successful and have a family at the same time. In the past few years, I haven't seen people who follow that line of thought. It may be the result of the women's movement, but I think women today are more open to choices.

I think it is better to work in your twenties and have children in your thirties. I enjoyed my pregnancy much more because I wasn't young enough to be wondering what I was missing. I didn't feel I was missing out on anything.

Having children gave Sandy the opportunity for a different direction in her life. Since she had been working, she welcomed the distractions of caring for her children. She never doubted that leaving her career temporarily was the right decision. She opted not to try to juggle motherhood and a career until she felt secure about being a mother. "I really enjoyed the baby stage best of all. After I came to understand myself, I knew I had to make a choice for a couple of years. When the baby got a little older, she understood that when I left, I would return."

Sandy is trying to change the attitudes perpetuated by tradition by raising her daughters to be prepared to make choices. She allows them the independence to make choices as they grow up: "I encourage them to do what they want to do. I want them to be pleased with themselves and not worry about always having the approval of me or others around them."

There are advantages and disadvantages to late parenthood. Knowing yourself as a person and possessing a degree of maturity helps you appreciate the wonder of growing children in a way apart from still growing up yourself. Older parents may have more financial security and thus may be more at ease themselves about raising children. This may be partially manifested in greater patience toward the long-awaited child. On the other side, heavy expenses of children in college tend to coincide with diminished earnings. Some older parents have also reported at age fifty an urge for the empty nest—a desire to return to the solitude and freedom from responsibility. This is of course difficult with teenagers in a household.

Late parenthood allows time in the twenties to establish a life before starting a family. Older parents are more fully aware of what they are missing and they have made the choice.

Early parenthood, too, has its set of advantages and disadvantages.

The primary disadvantage is usually economic. Young parents are stretched financially for homes, furniture, cars, new responsibilities, and other expenses at an economically low period in their career. They also experience social pressures to "keep up" their life as it existed prior to the introduction of a baby. Thus, it is easy for young parents to feel restricted by a child more often than blessed. The emotional maturity may not be present to assess the situation realistically. The advantages are definite; having the last child in school by age thirty; having large amounts of freedom by age forty, and having college tuition finished before income declines. Young mothers have their children to enjoy and their careers ahead. Though they may have missed some career advantages in establishing themselves early, young mothers are willing to accept this trade-off for the uninterrupted career progression in their thirties and forties.

A thirty-three-year-old mother of three reflects on the timing of her children.

> I had my first baby at twenty after I had married at nineteen. I was much too young and obviously the baby was not planned. However, I was too young for a career anyway and I worked on my college education around childcare arrangements. The handicaps that I had were in having to give up the social life I saw my unmarried friends enjoying. I never got the opportunity to participate in college clubs or anything of that nature. I just went to classes and came home. My husband was twenty-one and he dropped out of school to work, though my father offered to pay his tuition. He really wasn't much of a student and wasn't interested in earning a degree.
>
> I didn't know anything about being a mother but I knew I would not have an abortion even though I was not particularly happy about being pregnant. So I had a baby girl and she and I have grown up together. I finished college at the same time as my friends though I moved back to the town where my parents lived and transferred to another school. I never regained the friendships I lost among my college friends. As a couple, we had almost no married friends, certainly none with a child. My husband still lived as though he were single. His friends were the same and he went out with them all the time while I stayed home alone. I resented it very much.

She remembers the marriage was not terribly stable in those early years as she and her husband struggled with maturity and responsibility.

The situation seemed hopeful after a separation and reconciliation until she found out she was pregnant again.

That was during the Senate hearings on the birth-control pill. What I heard scared me so much that I quit taking the pill and counted the days on the calendar. About the third month I was pregnant. I was even more scared with the second pregnancy because I had a good job teaching school and I didn't want to give it up. I was just beginning to establish myself and the school policies at that time stated that a pregnant female had to leave after the fourth month. I lied about my due date so I could stay longer. My husband was so upset about the pregnancy that he said he was going to leave me. I begged him to stay with me until the baby was born. He reluctantly agreed.

As time progressed, this couple seemed to be more compatible, and when the second baby came, they rejoiced. He was twenty-four and she was twenty-three. The marriage eventually ended because the couple had different values, and she seemed to accept the responsibilities of parenthood as priority whereas he continued to live with a single-minded lifestyle.

She later remarried after going back to school for a graduate degree and was busy again trying to establish herself professionally when her second husband wanted to have a child.

I really enjoyed the two children I had, though I would not deny that I felt restricted. I just accepted that as a trade-off for early motherhood. But I tried to put all that behind me and look ahead. I knew I didn't want to be forever living in the past and thinking about what I had missed. When I remarried, I felt very secure about myself, personally, as a mother and professionally. I was finally advancing in my career and I received a marvelous opportunity to become the director of an educational center after graduate school. My new husband wanted to move west and I consented. I gave up the job opportunity to move with him. Then I felt an obligation to take some time getting the two children adjusted to a new city, new home, and new school, so I didn't get a job. After a year of adjustment, I decided to go ahead and have the baby for this marriage because my husband wanted it so much. And I was happy with him except that I really saw my career going out the window. I had a miscarriage and had to wait a few months and so I was twenty-nine when my third child was born. I think I was the oldest woman in the maternity ward but I felt like an old pro by this time. I had mixed emotions toward the very young first-time mothers I saw in the hospital. At first I thought, "Oh God, they don't know what lies ahead," and then I felt a tiny bit of envy for the naivety, the newness of such a fresh experience. Both emotions put me back in time and I realized how conflicting my own feelings were about the time to have a baby.

The third child was the only one of the three that was planned, and the mother doted on each stage of the baby's development. "I don't know if it was the third-child syndrome or if it was because I was older, but I loved having that third baby." The other two children were old enough to help with the baby and were quite protective of their new baby sister. Asked if she would recommend having the first baby so young, she replied,

I don't think many women could handle it; not that I could either but at that time contraception wasn't acceptable for good girls—I mean it implied planning. But times have changed and I don't really think there is a great benefit in having a child as young as I was. Growing up together is fun in a way, and it's fun for your child to have a young mother. But you never really forget the sacrifices you made and what you missed while you were at home with a baby. I can't remember a time when I wasn't a mother.

The Decision Is Final

Many women who have delayed having children have arrived at this family timing pattern through deliberate and carefully planned means. They have consciously analyzed their goals in life and their progress toward those goals each year. Making the decision to postpone parenting is usually seen as an investment toward realizing those goals.

However, once the decision is made to have a child, the impact on a woman's life is tremendous. Most women experience feelings of anticipation along with anxiety and excitement. The sense of change is overwhelming. Many use this motivating force to make changes, such as moving to a larger house or apartment, redecorating a room, or painting the entire house to get ready for the baby's arrival (as if the baby will notice). The transition is strong, however, and these feelings give way to bursts of energy to accomplish the tasks at hand. Emotional changes are also a strong sensation, and some women capitalize on these emotions to strengthen or reorder a relationship.

Whether a woman is having her first child or fourth, she often projects ahead and wonders, "What will my child be like?" Many imagine faceless babies. Some imagine the clean, sweet-smelling Gerber baby or other babies from media advertisements. Some prospective mothers have visions of apprehension about the appearance and development of their babies but this is a common occurrence. In looking ahead, an expectant mother projects many of the traditional contingencies upon herself. She may compare herself to the media mother who has her life in perfect order. She may wonder secretly whether or not she can live up to that standard. A woman may be disappointed when she compares her figure to that of the model who, wearing the latest in maternity apparel, never appears nauseous, swollen, or overweight.

The discrepancy between the expectations of pregnancy and childbirth and the reality of the experience is often unforeseen. A woman may be surprised in the reality unless she prepares through study or classes for childbirth. The controlled, quiet woman reclining on the delivery table is not real. A woman may feel strained and guilty for wanting to scream. Yet, many doctors can make a woman feel that she is the only one who has ever screamed by underestimating the pain and agony endured in the childbirth process. Women have a right to scream and to do so furiously. There is no other pain like childbirth, but there is no other joy like bringing a long-awaited child into the world.

The joys and pains of birth are many and varied. From the first twinge of nausea in the first weeks of pregnancy to the last excruciating pain of delivery, childbirth is a series of feelings that are never forgotten yet tend to slip from memory to oblivion. The details stand ready and waiting to be pulled out of storage on a moment's notice.

Becoming a parent does not begin with the birth of a child, nor with the germination of the seed. The expression which a child represents is a decision to alter and extend one's life. The choice is not an easy one to make, nor is it a choice which can be viewed in isolation from the sum total of life. The interaction which is involved and the fusing of personalities, routines, and directions for life are an integral part of becoming a parent.

ADJUSTING TO THE
CHANGING ROLE

In past times, motherhood has been referred to as the "sacred mission" or "woman's highest calling." This phraseology was the product of a patriarchal society which relied on the home as a basis for business interest and the female as its employee. Society was somewhat threatened by women who chose other terms for defining their lives. Patriarchy could not survive without motherhood as an unquestioned and unenlightened institution. Motherhood could at that time be paralleled with a truism such as the structure of the universe in order to close the door officially to the question of tolerating alternatives for women.

In early America, a typical family consisted of a dozen or more children. When population increases were a determining factor in the establishment of a new nation, the calling of women was compared to a patriotic love of country and the advancement of society. Motherhood was one giant step for mankind in America during the pioneer days.

The suffering of woman was purposive. She was bringing forth new life as a means of reproducing cities and colonies, thus providing the threads for binding a new nation. Without new life, there would be no expansion and continuation of families. Prosperity would pass to strangers, possibly barbarians. The woman was the center of purposes made by others which she took as her own goals. To bring forth a new governor, a soldier, or a clergyman was motivation enough for a woman to have her body swollen annually. Her suffering and pain were her value in the world.

Whatever the reason behind the decision to have a child, the task remains the same. Producing the child and directing the care which ensues is a collossal undertaking. The experiences of pregnancy, childbirth, and childcare are a series of both predictable and unpredictable crises. The demands brought about by such experiences and the effects on the physical and emotional stability of a woman are extremely taxing. Many women are not fully prepared to change to the extent that such experiences demand. Much of the required change involves the way the woman has seen herself, and the way others have seen her and her lifestyle. Her role by necessity must undergo tremendous adjustments. Part of the adjustment is prior to the birth of the child and part is after the child is at home when the responsibilities are assumed for a new life.

Certain aspects of femaleness have been glorified by society. In times past, the ability of a female to bear a child was revered. Contemporary society has placed a certain positive value on the physical attributes of a female. She is to look glamorous and appealing like a movie star. Within a short period of time, a woman is expected to have the body of a young girl again. Other societies take pride in certain rites of passage which transform a boy into a man. Yet our society does not accept the effects of childbirth on the female body as the passage from girlhood to womanhood. There is a great deal of conflict created by the media messages of voluptuous bodies and female attractiveness. Yet there is no recognition of the normal sacrifices of stretched skin and muscles which leave permanent marks and varicose veins from the harboring of an extra person. The host of physical changes which can occur as the result of pregnancy are neither welcome nor accepted. Women are left confused by the reality of their bodies and their situations as compared to the expectations they had brought into the role of mother.

Part of the adjustment to the changing role of parent lies in the acceptance of the appearance of the woman. The adjustment is usually more difficult as the pregnancy progresses. The role of mother suddenly becomes obvious to everyone just as if it had been announced. Most mothers who are excited about the coming event are proud of the first signs of "showing". They will shop for maternity clothes long before necessary, and they will anxiously await the evidence of their changing life before a mirror. A protruding stomach is the initiation into the world of adulthood and parenthood. As the protrusion enlarges, however, the self-image grows emotionally more negative. Though femininity is certainly not in doubt during this period, a woman often needs reassurance about her physical attractiveness. She knows she looks and feels like an elephant, but she still wants to hear, "You are beautiful." Women have been taught that unless they are beautiful and desirable, a man will not love them. Thus, most women are fearful of losing not only their figures but also their desirability in the process.

Even though many women fantasize about having a baby, the reality of conception still comes as a shock. Perhaps it seems like such a short time since she was a girl herself and suddenly she is no longer a girl. She is forever a different person when a new life grows within her. She hears jokes about her "condition." For those women who are unprepared for this transition, acceptance of the changing role may be even more difficult. Others who have planned and prepared themselves for this decision experience less shock through a mixture of feelings of wonder, bewilderment, and excitement. In *The Experience of Childbirth*, Kitzinger discusses the psychology of pregnancy.

> *The role of mother was previously seen only in others; but now the girl is called upon, relentlessly forced by the growing child inside her, to act a part she does not know, a part at once familiar and frightening.*[1]

The process of adjustment includes the husband as well as the wife. A new father must be willing to see his wife shift her attentions and her energies. He must be prepared not only to support those efforts but also to share fully in his own active commitment. This involves an extended role for the male as well as the female.

What about the myth of men being inept at childcare? The real truth in many cases is that women refuse to give men a chance. The typical stereotype is the father who sticks the baby with diaper pins, spills milk and food all over the unsuspecting child, and is totally helpless when the child cries. This stereotype has caused prejudice against men as participating fathers. Thus when he offers to help with the baby the wife says "Thanks, but no thanks. I'd rather do it myself." If he offers to "relieve" her of the household chores, she projects into her crystal ball and sees visions of dust behind the chairs and cobwebs in the untouched corners and she promptly changes the subject. Women see this area of responsibility as one of unclaimed power and authority—the one thing men have not claimed to achieve better than women. They are reluctant to open it to men and, as a result, many husbands are left out of the daily parenting cycle. Women have kept the responsibilities for themselves and the duties are dealt out by invitation only.

The idea that fathers are not interested in newborns is also a myth. This is another fallacy which has grown out of tradition. It had always been a woman's responsibility to care for a new baby. Fathers have had to keep at arms length. After all fathers are big and clumsy and babies are tiny and fragile. In actuality fathers can be quite capable in the physical care of children if given the chance to learn and perform.

Many contemporary women are moving away from tradition in ways which open the door to a partnership arrangement in parenting. More

---

[1] Sheila Kitzinger, *The Experience of Childbirth* (New York: Viking Penguin, Inc., 1972), p. 54.

women let their husbands know that from the beginning they expect the child to have two equal parents. Basic care of the child can be shared to the benefit of both parents and the child if the parents agree philosophically about sharing the demands of parenthood.

New fathers have traditionally excluded themselves or have been excluded from active participation in the care of the children. Both men and women have expected lesser participation from men. Culturally, childcare has been considered inferior or unmasculine. The role of the male has been to provide and to appreciate. Some men do not assert their hidden desires to share in full parenting because they are embarrassed that their performance may be inadequate. For the first time in the marriage men may feel inadequate, and it is disconcerting to acknowledge the existence of such feelings. There is a significant male adjustment process following the birth of a child, and understanding these emotions can clarify many confusing experiences for men and women.

Gail had been a librarian and had chosen not to have children. But at thirty-six she got pregnant for the first time because her husband, Jim, wanted a child. After the birth, Gail found that although her schedule had changed considerably, she enjoyed her new role as a mother. Her husband took his role of father seriously. Since he had been the one to convince his wife to have a child, Jim asserted his paternalism by feeding, rocking, cuddling, bathing, and playing with the baby. He shopped and cleaned. He did more than help. Since he felt the child was a shared responsibility, Jim did not feel it was Gail's duty to assume the primary caretaker role. He did not feel that he was "helping" her. Rather Jim believed that each parent should share all aspects of the parenting process. He encouraged Gail to remain active in her work since she had expressed that desire.

Jim and Gail were in agreement about the physical effects of childbirth. Neither expected Gail to have the body of a young girl. She had collected a few extra pounds during pregnancy and nursing and she felt her baby was extremely healthy because of her careful nutrition. She was casual in her attitude about childcare. She dressed and behaved accordingly. Gail was not bothered if her hair was slightly windblown or her shoes were not the latest style. Jim accepted her the way she was. When she became pregnant the second time, she was wearing braces on her teeth and rethinking her ordering of life which she had previously felt so sure about. "It's so hard to have everything you really think you want out of life." She now speaks from the wisdom that comes only from experience. "It's hard to get it all." Gail spoke about her feelings regarding trade-offs for a mother. She was very much a strong advocate of women getting paid what they are worth—even though she knew that in her position, her skills much exceeded her job. "Women are too willing to make sacrifices in order to have the schedule they want. They are giving up bargaining power for better pay because so many employers know they can get a part-time mother-worker who will work for so little just to keep herself active. It hurts in the long run yet I am guilty, too."

Most mothers experience some type of sacrifice in deciding to have a child. For many, that sacrifice involves career. Whether it is a shift to part-time work, a slowing down, or a reluctance to accept additional responsibilities, the effect may be to impair the success of her career. At the very least of possible effects is the set-back of women behind their male counterparts and behind childfree women in the work force. Just as Gail realized the impact of a willingness to work short hours for low pay, so working mothers know they are overtrained and underpaid. Yet they are freely inclined to continue such situations because of their desire to keep their careers alive.

One set of conflicts gives birth to another. Women want to prolong their professional self-esteem throughout the experience of pregnancy and motherhood. To do so, they are willing to compromise and sacrifice just to "stay in the game." They are afraid of having to sit on the bench as a permanent spectator when they have been playing a key position. Women hang on desperately to the only role they have known. They are torn between the known world of work and self-reliance and the unknown world of "sacred calling" and "fulfillment." Many are afraid to leave one world behind because they cannot yet see themselves as a changed person across the threshold in the new world of motherhood. The role adjustments are extremely difficult.

Be Prepared

A husband can be very supportive during the period of rapid changes which occur from pregnancy through birth and even into the specific ways in which he can share this experience more openly while simultaneously showing support for his wife.

A man can show support for the adjustments his wife is having to make through demonstration of his interests in the events taking place. During pregnancy, it is important for the woman to feel desired and attractive. No one is in a better position to do this than the one who is closest to her, the partner of her new experience. He can visit the doctor with his wife; read books and articles on pregnancy and childcare; go to classes on birth and parenting; and help the woman with exercises and relaxation. He can also discuss with sensitivity what his wife is feeling. Additional assistance in sharing household routines shows an attitude of togetherness and awareness of her physical demands.

Occassionally, a pregnant woman may experience emotionally or physically low periods. She may be easily upset by comments or actions from unsupporting relatives or friends. In such instances, a man can help her through such periods of adjustment by acting as a liaison between her and any negative feelings which she may experience. He can boost those emotional lows and raise her sagging self-concept by surprising her unexpectedly with particular consideration or gifts. A partnership pregnancy helps a woman through the varied and difficult adjustments which accompany the decision to enter the unknown world of parenthood.

Psychologically as well as physically, this is a period of great change. The mother may feel tied down with maternity and domesticity even though she might have chosen this route. She may be struggling with tasks for which she has little or no training and which recur day by day with monotonous regularity.

The child, though loved and cared for, may occasionally provoke feelings of resentment or extreme irritation. Although most mothers admit to a broad spectrum of emotions, they rarely expect negative feelings to occur, though it may be a hidden fear. Prior to the baby's birth, a prospective mother is bombarded with books, advertisements, and media presentations of obviously happy and healthy babies. These babies are hardly comparable to the new red-faced, wrinkled, crying arrival. A mother may look at her own baby and see scaly scalp, diaper rash, peeling skin, boney feet, birth marks, and unfocused eyes. What, she asks herself, did she do wrong? She feels guilty and somewhat of a failure for nonfulfillment of her dreams to produce a pin-up baby. She also feels awkward about even comparing her own little bundle with that of an advertisement, not to mention showing a preference.

A new mother soon realizes that babies change in their looks and manage to turn into children who for some strange reason resemble their mother or father or both. It does happen, and mothers, though impatient, are advised to relax and accept nature as it develops. A new mother must learn to know and love her baby just as he or she is. This is the first step in knowing him or her as a person. Disconcerting feelings which go unexplained become a source of anxiety and actually feed on the mother's own supply of mental and physical energy.

Motherhood brings many changes for a woman who has chosen to enter its ranks. Inherent in the experience are demands and changes with which a woman will be faced. Some of the adjustments are more difficult to accept than others.

The process of birth requires some mental adjustments prior to its onset. Men have not only guided women into motherhood but also taken control over the birth process. Adrienne Rich writes in *Of Women Born* that women are expected to be passive sufferers and that physicians have capitalized on this in directing the command of the childbirth process to themselves rather than to the women. As a result, women have learned to doubt their ability to trust themselves ultimately and have transferred this power to men.[2] Many are led to believe they simply cannot act on their instincts, particularly in regard to natural childbirth. Mothers have had taken away from them the climax of their decision to have children. The birth of a woman's baby is controlled in many cases by a male, who is telling her to go to sleep and let him take over. Such men are thieves of the banner of motherhood. They deny women their right to be the primary power in the birth process.

Regina recalled some of the experiences of her pregnancy:

I wasn't really ready for a baby, but when I felt nauseous for several mornings and afternoons, I accepted the inevitable. After the pregnancy was confirmed I told my husband immediately and he was shocked. I had always dreamed of something more romantic—like a candlelight dinner where I would set an obviously empty third place. It wasn't very romantic because he was even less prepared for a baby than I, but after a short time we both were excited. It was really strange that I would have been upset in the least because we had talked of having children before we married. There was never any doubt that I would be a mother, but suddenly it was no longer a fantasy, a girlhood dream of the past.

I read everything I could on pregnancy and birth. I read books and enrolled in Lamaze classes. I focused on my body and couldn't envision

[2]Adrienne Rich, *Of Woman Born* (New York: W.W. Norton & Co., 1976), pp. 151-52, 171-72.

beyond the birth. I was absorbed with what was occuring inside my womb. I remember how nauseous I was—how we had to stop the car so often. I remember how overcome with sleep I would feel. I was always looking at pictures of babies, reading about babies, or shopping around for baby things.

The delivery wasn't all that difficult. It really hurt but the doctor insisted I take something for pain. I have since learned to resent that domination. It was easier on him for me to be asleep and still. That way, he could pull the baby out, stamp it "O.K." then send me a bill. I wanted to give birth and have my husband involved but the doctor wouldn't bend his tradition even though we had taken the childbirth classes. The next thing I knew I was groggy, lying in the recovery room hearing, "We've got a big girl," I couldn't believe it was a girl because I was so sure it was a boy. I thought in my dizziness that perhaps they hadn't looked closely enough! I remember asking two questions, "Are you sure?" and "Is she OK?"

As the weeks went on I felt scared and alone—even though I wasn't really alone. I guess it was the baby blues. I felt like I had lost my figure, my self-image, my job, my economic independence, and my free association with adults. I felt stranded and I knew there was no turning back. Yet I didn't seriously want to turn back. The attachment I felt to my baby daughter was tremendous, but the emotional upheaval was unexpected and confusing.

Other adjustments are more positive experiences and thus more readily integrated into a woman's nature. There are many affirmative changes which can be attributed to becoming a mother. Motherhood may put one more in touch with practical reality by giving one a special alertness or sensitivity to others. A woman may experience a sense of softness after she has become a mother.

Rich expressed the changes that women experience in expanding their self-concept.

Many women are expressing the sense that at this moment in human history it is simply better to be a woman; that the broadening and deepening of the demand for women's self-determination has created a largeness of possibility, a scope for original thought and activism, above all a new sense of mutual aims and sharing among women; that we are living on the edge of immense changes which we ourselves are creating.[3]

Women are opening to the possibilities of choice, not dictates. In allowing women to choose the direction of their lives, society is beginning to see women realistically, as individuals rather than traditional role-bearers. And women themselves are willing to change their roles in whatever direction they choose.

AFTERBIRTH PAINS
OF ISOLATION

A woman is usually pampered before giving birth, and so she should be. Any woman who has experienced pregnancy knows how difficult it is to spend nine months as a living garden while the "seed" grows into another person. Any pregnant woman can relate how hard it is to expand from the Atlantic to the Pacific before your very eyes—to wonder for weeks and weeks if your feet are still there. But afterwards, when the baby is born, when she has the hardest work to do, no one sings her praises. She is left alone with a baby and a growing sense of isolation. It is too easy to slide into a perpetual routine wherein a mother is drowning in housework and baby work. Though she may be there by choice, she may at the same time be losing confidence she once had about herself as an individual and about her professional career.

Some new mothers do not want to leave their new babies at all. Mothers have described their feelings regarding leaving their baby in terms of conflict. These feelings are not so much of guilt as a sense of loss. They miss every moment not spent with the child. As a result they are hesitant about spending time in entertainment. They do not want to be absent from the baby and so they choose staying at home as opposed to going out with friends. The emotional tug of motherhood becomes a struggle between old routines and new desires.

Postpartum depression is another emotion not to be overlooked. After birth, from a period of several days to several weeks (or even months in some cases), a mother experiences an emotionally low feeling. Pregnancy was in itself a series of ups and downs physically and emotionally. It

---

[3]*Ibid.,* p. 203.

was climaxed by the actual birth of the long-awaited baby. But after the birth is over and the mother is at home, she is suddenly faced with awesome feelings of responsibility. She has been the center of attention for nine or ten months and she now feels alone and isolated. The baby has taken over as the star attraction, and the newness of the arrival has worn off and she is on her own.

Rona, a successful market researcher, found motherhood far more difficult than her business career. She limited herself to part-time work because in the past she had been made to feel guilty for leaving her sons. She could have worked full time because she was well respected in her field. Her time was in demand. Yet she experienced the same conflicts about success and womanhood that many other women do.

I married early because I wanted to prove my womanhood. I had never dated much or been popular and so I guess I was anxious to confirm that part of my life. I had always excelled in male areas and so I never thought much about babies or role-playing motherhood with dolls. I had mixed feelings when I learned I was to be a mother, but after my first son was born, I was delighted to discover that I loved caring for a baby. This was contrary to all my expectations since I hated housework and cooking.

After the first year, my son became much harder to cope with. I left my job to spend all my time at home. I wondered about my instincts as a mother. Since I had quit work, I was alone with my thoughts and fears. I began to doubt myself as a mother, as a woman, and even as the competent, dependable person I had always known myself to be. I was a strong person yet this twelve-month-old child was causing me to doubt everything about myself. I would walk around the house thinking, "I can't stand this another hour." Yet, I knew he wasn't doing anything out of the ordinary for a superactive baby. I almost grieved over my feelings but I realized it wasn't good for me or the baby to be so isolated—when I really needed more contact and stimulation from the outside world.

Rona could have returned to work, even part time or with flexible hours, but she chose to stay at home. She felt torn about leaving the baby. "The baby doesn't know he needs me here all the time, and maybe he doesn't. But I tell myself, my baby needs me. Maybe I'm the one who needs my baby."

Changing Your Mind

Women are certainly known for changing their minds. No one seems to notice much when a man changes his mind, but with a woman it is different.

Career women who thought they were fully committed to a life without children may at a later time in life decide to have a child.

"My friends thought I had gone mad," said Freda a long-time feminist and career woman. "But I had reached the time in my life when I began to have other priorities besides my work. The idea of having a child became more and more appealing. The unique intimacy of childbirth was something that I didn't want to deny myself."

After her child was born, Freda found out how much her life had changed. Her friends no longer felt that she was "one of them." They stopped coming to see her and she stopped visiting them. She was warned that her career would end and that sooner or later she would regret it. She felt snubbed by her former colleagues, and so Freda found companionship among other new mothers.

Having a child opened my eyes to a great many things. I realized how many women, especially professional, highly motivated women, are fearful about becoming mothers. They are afraid of losing themselves, their identity, their professional image. They are afraid of taking on such unknown responsibilities and entering a new world. They are filled with fear about failure. They don't know if certain "natural" instincts are really there. What happens when they are alone with the baby and solely responsible for it? They are scared to death.

Talking to other mothers does help ease apprehensions that new mothers have. Other mothers can provide support, encouragement, and companionship. There is no pressure on a relationship that is based on the common bond of interest in children. "I found it much easier to talk to other mothers," Freda said. "Whereas, I had been such a feminist and hard-nosed career woman, I found myself with a completely new set of interests. Even my vocabulary changed. The birth of my baby transformed me. I see now what mothers experience and I have a new respect for mothers that I never had before."

For Freda, the sense of isolation turned out to be a positive force. She knew how to direct her needs to a new source, a fresh group of friends. Not all new mothers who choose to stay home are so fortunate.

For some mothers, the privacy of the home has facilitated isolation and loneliness. The new affluence which generated moves to the suburbs and larger private homes has caused a loss of neighborhood commonality and sharing of the mothering routines with other women. The sense of being housebound has increased. In order to have the enjoyment of a heretofore casual, unscheduled companionship with other mothers, times must now be organized. The spontaneity has given way to deliberateness. The isolation of the home has increased with the family's material success.

In the past, motherhood has been a matter of restricted choices. A woman had less control over her lifestyle and the number of children that were born to her. Her day-to-day activities were determined by what happened to her body. Some contemporary women, though possessing more control over the number of children born, remain in restricted environments. Some feminist writers have referred to these limitations as destructive.

> *What woman, in the solitary confinement of a life at home enclosed with young children, or in the struggle to mother them while providing for them single-handedly, or in the conflict of weighing her own personhood against the dogma that says she is a mother, first, last and always—what woman has not dreamed of "going over the edge," of simply letting go, relinquishing what is termed her sanity, so that she can be taken care of for once, or can simply find a way to take care of herself? The mothers: collecting their children at school; sitting in rows at the parent-teacher meeting; placating weary infants in the supermarket carriages; straggling home to make dinner, do laundry, and tend to children after a day at work; fighting to get decent care and livable schoolrooms for their children; waiting for child support checks while the landlord threatens eviction; getting pregnant yet again because their one escape into pleasure and abandon is sex; . . . wakened by a child's cry from their eternally unfinished dreams—the mothers, if we could look into their fantasies—their daydreams and imaginary experiences—we would see the embodiment of rage, of tragedy, of the overcharged energy of love, of inventive desperation . . .*[4]

The renewed hope of women for the future lies in the courage of

[4]*Ibid.*, p. 285.

women. They must trust in their instincts instead of feeling inadequate or abdicating power to men out of assumed weakness. Women are not lost, isolated creatures. They are strong enough to bring the creation and sustenance of life of another human being into the decision of conscious intelligence just as any work selectively determined. They are strong enough to repel isolation through an understanding of those emotions and a determination to direct those mental energies into productive courses.

HOW CAN I BE SO TIRED?

Casey had decided to stay home when Ann Marie was born. She had always dreamed of having a beautiful daughter and the time had finally come. However, Casey was unprepared for the real world of motherhood. She had pictured her baby as just like the babies on the television commercials—sweet, cooing, smiling, smelling clean and fresh. What a shock when Ann Marie had colic for five months! "Oh for a night of uninterrupted sleep!" Casey recalled. "What I would have given for some rest! I was constantly attending to the baby's needs. When I wasn't with her directly, I had to be washing clothes, sterilizing bottles, and making formula for her supplemental feedings or sorting diapers. I never had a minute to myself. My life had never been anything like this."

After several weeks of this rigid routine, Casey felt fatigued and began to feel depressed. She loved the baby very much and certainly took pleasure in looking after her but she felt like another person—not the Casey she had known for twenty-seven years. She felt mothering was giving her no ego rewards. "No one," she concluded, "could possibly know how much I give of myself to be a mother." It was even more difficult for her because she had always been extremely active in pursuit of her own interests. She was a scholarship winner in literature and had done some writing. She had been very active in remodeling a Victorian house even until the day Ann Marie was born. Now there was no time left for Casey, and even if there was, Casey simply did not have the energy.

Fatigue is definitely a problem of pregnancy and new motherhood. Both put a tremendous strain on the mother's body. The task of actually growing another human being and caring for that new person is monumental, and for this assignment extra rest is needed.

The feelings of utter fatigue may cause other conflicts. A woman may be short-tempered, unaffectionate, and insensitive because she is overly tired. Some women push themselves even harder to show they "can do it." This is unwise Help is needed from husbands, relatives, friends, or paid assistants.

As much excitement as there is over pregnancy, there are also some real difficulties. One of those is clearly physical. Few prospective mothers are so fortunate as to avoid morning sickness. Almost none avoid fatigue. The feeling of being extremely tired continuously haunts expectant mothers. Before birth, a pregnant woman may feel totally exhausted from a simple task such as peeling a potato. Sleep may call so loudly that a woman cannot possibly ignore its pull.

There are many high and low points of energy during the period before motherhood. Many women think they are going to continue feeling listless for the rest of their days. The fatigue is so strong and the demands of pregnancy are so great that for the first time in their lives women cannot depend on inner strength for a reliable support system. The hormonal and physical shifting of childbearing are enormous. Even in the healthiest of pregnancies, there are feelings of loss of self and of giving your total being to another. It is essentially a sufferance, an experience of no longer being in complete control over your body.

New mothers feel the physical and emotional stress of parenthood particularly if they are breastfeeding. Nursing mothers need even more rest in order to avoid tension and fatigue which can inhibit the nursing process.

New mothers also have strong emotions about caring for their babies. They are afraid to leave the baby with anyone so soon and the strong bonds of attachment between mother and baby add to their hesitancy to be away. A new mother often feels extremely possessive about caring for the baby. Consequently, even when help is available, she strongly prefers taking care of the child herself.

It is not unusual for a new mother to have to change her plans for return to work after she discovers how continuously tired she is. The struggle to maintain a job while being a new mother is extremely difficult physically and emotionally. Those mothers who have to work need additional support from relatives and friends during this period of time.

Some mothers love to be busy; they are in a constant state of activity. Women like this have high energy levels and large amounts of determination. They sometimes, but not in all cases, have a great ability to tolerate frustration. They look at homemaking as a challenge to coordinate hundreds of details for several people into one smooth operation.

Other mothers can barely manage the minimum of housework, meal planning, organization of family routines, and childcare. They feel tired and unable to cope with large doses of future thinking.

Effects of Fatigue

Many women are aware of the effects of fatigue on a relationship. Most have either experienced this firsthand or know personally of someone who has. The situation is that of the amorous husband who has had a satisfying workday and a good home-cooked meal, has read the paper, and watched television, and is ready to go to bed—but not to sleep. The focus then turns to the wife. She has supervised dough-making and painting, given the children naps, cooked breakfast, worked toddler puzzles, picked up toys, vacuumed, dusted, made beds, done three loads of laundry, read stories, gone grocery shopping with two small children, pushed them in swings, prepared lunch and dinner, cleaned the kitchen three times, and just as she makes her final rounds to pick up the clutter in the family room before exhaustion knocks her off her feet, her husband says that he is ready for bed. She feels like saying plenty, but usually she is just too tired and consents. But he wonders what has happened to that old spark of enthusiasm that used to surround their love-making. She does not communicate about his lack of understanding. She feels he would only get angry because "this is her job." But he works only eight hours and she works sixteen in addition to being "on call" during the night.

A child is a selfish being. It has no regard for a mother's feelings of fatigue. It can actually increase tension in the relationship. Many husbands feel excluded. They may call from the office during the day and the wife may respond, "I'm too busy with the baby to talk right now." She may say, "I'll have to call you back," and the time does not come. The husband receives a clear message. The baby comes first.

The spontaneity of an intimate relationship is also affected. Suddenly, the time together must be planned around feedings or outings. A certain freedom of expression as an adult is traded for parenthood.

Vickie remembers, "In the early days of tending the baby, I was so tired. When James came home from work, instead of handing him the newspaper I handed him the baby. We used to enjoy quiet, candlelit dinners. When I could muster enough energy after the baby was born to prepare a quiet dinner for the two of us, it seemed we would always be interrupted by cries."

Lack of enthusiasm is not really a reflection on a relationship or a marriage per se. The point is that the woman is worn out and in her order of priorities, the needs of the children are more pressing than adult needs. It is a demanding life and many women (and men too, if role reversal were true to expectation) cannot continually tolerate such demands.

Mothers, especially new mothers, are very tired and quite pre-occupied with a baby. This does not mean any less love toward their husband, but it does mean that temporarily the husband seems to stand in line for attention. Many men do not understand this and consequently become angry that their wives are not willing to put everything else aside for them. This lack of understanding or lack of maturity adds to the difficulty a mother already feels. This is one of the primary reasons new parents experience marital strains. The relationship must be mature enough for each partner to realize what is happening and why.

A husband who is hurt by his wife's lack of attention may try to get back at her by saying or doing something he knows will upset her. In doing that, he knows he will most assuredly get her attention. Some wives report their husbands act like little boys or take everything personally. Unless the husband is considerate and mature enough (there is no age limit to immaturity; it is a mental condition) to share the period of new parent-hood with the mother, the strains are apt to pull them apart. Thus the woman finds herself mothering her husband as well as her child. The idea of having children to improve a weak marriage is foolish because children bring so many claims into a relationship. If that relationship is fragile, it will not withstand the demands of needs outside the couple.

There are many ways to show love between husband and wife when demands are excessive for one or the other. The willingness to try to understand the situation is the first step in supportive love. The next is helping. Though a husband may feel rejected by his weary wife, he will most assuredly gain in her affections if he helps lessen her tension. Rather like a helpmate instead of a rival for the baby, the husband can and should share in the child's care. Through togetherness, then, a couple can be drawn closer and realize that they are showing love to each other by many of the things they do.

Fatigue can also be manifested through mental depression. Most mothers are familiar with postnatal depression, but some mothers have claimed it hit during pregnancy and lasted for years. Mental depression may go undiagnosed while the health of the mother, the welfare of the child, and the depth of feelings in a marriage are all harmfully affected.

The fatigue of mothering can be shown in other ways. Although depression can occur because a mother is overly tired, a sense of selfhood may also diminish when a mother finds little opportunity for time alone. Solitude is a basic human need—a time to reflect, to regroup one's thoughts. A person who is busy doing things for others needs to have some time alone.

Some women enjoy going to the hairdresser regularly just to have time to themselves, to feel pampered and renewed. Others enjoy shopping, sewing, art, music, or reading as opportunities to get away from continuous demands. Many women enjoy gardening or cooking as their outlet. A few women (though they must surely be traveling with loose marbles) actually enjoy housecleaning. All women need to have some outlet for getting away or regrouping or just relaxing alone.

Need for Rest
and Renewal

Childbirth and infant care are usually underestimated in terms of physical output. Many new mothers fail to anticipate how much rest will be needed for the maintenance of their own strength. The process of birth and the ensuing weeks and months of care are far more exhausting than most mothers dream, especially if they have a cranky baby or one who is particularly active. Unfortunately, this cannot be accurately predicted in advance, though some may guess that all that excessive kicking in the womb may be signs of the energy ahead.

Mothers are quickly exhausted from getting up several times a night and from the work of constant care. There is never enough time to recover fully in order to be prepared for the next twenty-four hours. Few mothers are fortunate enough to have babies who sleep all night without waking to be fed during the first few weeks of life. Later the child may awaken for water or comfort which may continue the pattern of interrupted sleep for years.

The fatigue experienced by many women is overwhelming. It cannot be predicted and it can deplete even the most vigorous of women. Some have reported periods of eating nothing but take-out food or frozen dinners. Others recall letting the house turn to dust and the plants die. Many say they felt barely able to nurture the baby and themselves.

Pregnancy and childbirth is a tough physical job, and the daily and nightly demands of feeding, caring, holding, rocking and bathing are physically exhausting. There is an emotional and physical basis for fatigue.

One woman recalled,

When I was pregnant I felt more tired than I had ever felt in my entire life. But when the baby was born, I was 100 percent more tired. I know there is an emotional letdown after the arrival; the routine is somewhat unsettling. But I slowed down in my thinking. I was just too tired to do anything. It seemed a big effort to call a sitter. I was too tired to pick up a book. The simplest daily routines became a production. I was really too tired to bundle up the baby for a stroll, but somehow I managed to function.

When new fathers assume a role of active involvement, they too can experience physical stress. Many fathers are willing to assist in a partnership of parenting if they are given the opportunities by the mother. Fathers who have taken over night feedings for example relate how rewarding intrinsically it was for them to have those quiet hours in the night to feed, rock, and hold their babies. They grow in the bonding process as the attachment between father and child strengthens. Unfortunately, male colleagues and employers are not sympathetic to participating fathers. A father may love the nights spent cuddling his baby yet feel inhibited about admitting he had done such "woman's work." Men may inwardly feel coerced into hiding their true emotions. They may put on a strong appearance at the office especially during a hard day when they feel wiped out and know there is no compassion among their fellows.

Often men feel embarrassed about their emotionality, their intense feelings for the baby, and their desire to share in childcare. At the same time they may be ambivalent over seeing their wives' attention totally shifted to the little intruder. Fathers may feel that they are shut out from their wives' and their babies' lives. All these feelings cause a great deal of stress and emphasize the need for emotional support for fathers and mothers alike.

In time, confidence, security, and strength are renewed, and tensions and pressures lessen. Before this period of emotional and physical turmoil for the father and mother, the mother's body was doing all the work and all the caretaking. Since child-rearing has traditionally been seen as woman's domain, she is expected to be confident and relaxed. However, neither the mother nor the father is superhuman in reality and some degree of fatigue and emotional upheaval is normal and expected.

A woman bears the pains of birth and she feels isolated, tired, and confused over her conflicting emotions as she makes the ultimate and irrevocable decision to become a mother. An understanding of the underlying emotions beneath these conflicts can help a woman work through those difficult periods and can provide further insight into the reality of the everyday world of motherhood. Clarifying these perceptions improves the capacity of a woman to be all that she can be, relieved of unknown, unexpected and unrecognized anxieties.

5

The Decision: Giving Up the Job

CONTEMPORARY ATTITUDES about working mothers and the influence of the women's movement affect those women who do not work as well as those who do. Many women who have chosen not to work, whether temporarily or for an extended period of time, feel defensive about staying home. There is a moment of awkwardness when a woman is asked what she does and if she works. A mother who stays home may feel defensive. Who is the more productive person? A homemaker may want to say that she is not wasting her time or losing her mental abilities. She may feel frustrated to the extent that she wants to say to working women, "I have chosen an alternate lifestyle. I'm just as bright as you are, but I'm staying home." In the last analysis, the fine line is choice—the choice to determine the priority or most appropriate direction for each individual.

The decision to give up a job or put a career on hold is usually one of the most difficult decisions a woman makes. Many women have postponed having children for years because they could not make the decision. Others are afraid that once they have stopped their careers they may not be able to reenter at the same point, especially in the competitive job market. Even worse, they feel exclusion altogether from the professional ranks. What if, they might ask themselves, I do not like staying at home? Many women are afraid to risk being trapped; afraid of possible resentment toward the baby for tying them down.

The realism of strained economics is a haunting fear for women who project possible changes in economic conditions. The uncertainty of life situations is a special concern for women who have left good jobs. They are insecure that doors which lead to employment opportunities will be permanently closed to them. The possible changes which loom over the heads of dependent women are frightening. A change in marital or financial conditions can provoke apprehensions in women that are both continuing and real.

Still, many women are ready and willing to give up a job or temporarily halt a career in order to devote themselves to their families. Often the women who make this decision have been conditioned early in their lives by tradition, and they have anticipated taking this step in their own future.

However, there is no rational reason for women to give up a career without compensation in some form. The trade-off may be entirely emotional, but the rewards should equally match the need for satisfaction which all women possess. Staying at home is not compensation per se. It must be accompanied by a system which provides gratification for those needs.

Some women choose to stay home without having a "baby" excuse. And why should they not have the freedom to choose? When a husband and wife determine this decision mutually and both are in agreement, they will share in the satisfaction and benefits which can be derived from their choice. Assuming that a relationship is based on mutual satisfaction, a couple in accord on this issue is less likely to experience conflict than a couple composed of one who favors staying home and one who does not.

WHO AM I NOW?

"Who am I now?" is a question many women answer with "I am a housewife." The response is almost apologetic. A woman who decides to give up a job or career is faced with many changes. Among those changes are perspectives about herself. After she becomes adjusted to the idea of staying home with or without the routines of childcare, she may settle back and wonder who and what she really is now that her life has changed so dramatically. She may call herself a full-time homemaker.

The terms *housewife* and *homemaker* are often used synonomously and both were thought to be occupational choices for women. The myth of women's place as exclusively in the home is a product of a period in which man had been displaced from the home as his place of work. The role of housewife emerged with the advent of industrialization. Both the roles of women and men were affected. Each changed to meet the demands of the social times. Man was leaving the house to work. His role was to accept the responsibility for all financial matters. The woman became the keeper of the house—the manager of the hearth.

With the exception of the socially inferior, most families had at least one servant. The life of domesticity into which married women "retired" actually involved no housework. Many women may have chosen the occupation for this reason, but the motive is indistinguishable in the history books.

Home roles were reorganized. Work was no longer done by families at home. Work and family life were separated. Labor was performed for money outside the home, which had nothing to do with family relationships or values.

> *The differentiation of the family from the economy necessitated by the changeover to industrial production was followed eventually by a differentiation of roles within the family. The woman became the non-employed, economically dependent housewife, and the man became the sole wage or salary earner, supporting by his labor his wife—the housewife and her children. This division of gender roles was incorporated into the ideals of the middle class in the first decades of the nineteenth century, and was increasingly put into practice among middle-class families until after the Second World War. The ideal only became part of working class culture at the beginning of this century.*[1]

This change at first was neither understood nor welcomed, and in the first textile mills, whole families would be hired, with the husband and father allocated to one job and the women and children to another. Children indeed learned their training as apprentices to their parents.

A woman factory worker not only posed the threat of competition for jobs but also risked the welfare of her infants and children by her separation from them. Separation prohibited the breastfeeding which was necessary for life. The death rate for infants was 50 to 80 percent because milk was contaminated and food was drugged with narcotics.[2]

[1] Ann Oakley, *Woman's Work: The Housewife, Past and Present* (New York: Pantheon Books, a division of Random House, Inc., copyright © 1976), p. 34.

[2] *Ibid.*, p. 48.

As factories flourished, industry became concentrated in certain areas, cutting off thousands of women in rural areas who earned money from outwork, primarily spinning. With no alternate work, women were faced with staying home. Women were expected to support themselves according to the working-class view. They were forced to take up other employment, usually domestic (as teachers, governesses, and servants). Women also did the agricultural work in times past.

Thus the duties of women evolved from changes in social conditions, and until the 1970s, the position seemed inerrant. The total thrust of the duties and responsibilities, even the purpose of women, was carried on from one generation to another and focused on the image of women at home. Socially there has been little distinction between the role of wife and mother and the role of housewife.

The Housewife Image

Many mothers at home are there by choice and feel quite fulfilled in their roles. They have no identity problems because they never lost the strong sense of selfhood which they brought into the choices they made. This is not true for all mothers and even for those who fit the description, permanency is no guarantee.

The image of the housewife, or homemaker, as many women prefer to be called, has been idealized through magazines, advertising, television, and short stories. There has been some element of glamor in the calling which appeals to women, and many hang onto that expectation for years though they may never experience its existence. A fatigued or over-burdened housewife may take refuge in those ideals which enable her to make contact with her ideal self: that part of her that seeks to be beautiful and efficient. She may be pushed by the expectation of her role in society to strive for perfection. The drive to achieve perfection and the comparison of self to the ideal carry inherent burdens of emotional conflict and distress.

Some mothers make life more difficult for themselves by perpetuating an idealized image of the self which is out of touch with the realities with which they must cope. This, in turn, causes them to suffer under the strain of trying to live up to an impossible ideal—the thin, glamorous mother who is perfectly organized, cleans her home in designer clothes, and never has a problem with her children. Such ideals of motherhood have been accumulated through books, baby experts, and the focus of the media on glamor and beauty. It is almost impossible for a mother to live up to such standards, yet she pushes herself to the limit in trying to achieve the ideal.

Many women have lost their identity as individuals while striving to live up to the virtuous homemaker image. In the 1970s there were more runaway wives reported than any time previously. Women have begun to ask themselves, "Is this all I can do? Is this the sum total of my worth?" They have expressed feelings of restriction on their inner beings whereas men are able to pursue their talents and interests with freedom. The result of this dilemma is tension and stress in women, some of whom turn to tranquilizing drugs or alcohol. Some have left their husbands and children "to find themselves."

One such woman is Jo Ann. She felt secure about her lifestyle and her goals. She was outspoken, artistic, and very creative, and though she had no formal training, she was able to find outlets for expressing herself through her art and activities outside the home. She often felt that other women were less interesting because they weren't really "doing anything."

"I don't like to hear mothers talk about nothing but potty training," Jo Ann would say after an encounter with other mothers. She felt alive and free until her husband began to push her toward a more traditional role as wife. She left Jack and when she did she left behind a daughter and a son. She left the state and seemed happy to have the chance to determine the direction of her life without restrictions.

Tradition has not prepared society to accept runaway wives and mothers. Most people react negatively to a woman who leaves or gives up a child. However, not all women are natural mothers and are therefore unwilling and unprepared to adjust their lives to accomodate the expectations with which they are faced. As a result, many are choosing openly to turn in the other direction—to shift parenting and childcare to the parent who seems more capable and willing to manage the needs of the children. More fathers are learning how to "mother," and many are shocked at the depth of maternal responsibilities. Men have not been conditioned to think through details that are inherent in childcare and home management, and many are gaining a new appreciation for the role of wife and mother.

Conflict:
Ideal and Real

How did they get lost? What happened along the way that caused these women to lose their sense of identity? First, women are conditioned to relate through other people. They relate as daughters through their parents, and unless they are independent by nature, they find a mate soon after leaving the care of their parents. The situation then reads—relate through your spouse. A woman usually goes from being Mr. and Mrs. Doe's daughter to being John Smith's wife. Her name changes from Jane Doe to Mrs. John Smith. Then she becomes Tom and Susie's mother. When does a woman get to be just Jane—as she is and wants to be? Unless Jane takes the time away from marriage, children, or family attachments and lives independently, she may never experience living alone and relating to others as Jane.

One such case of tradition and loss of identity is Ruth, age thirty-five, living in a large northern industrial city. Ruth got married two years after high school and worked as a secretary temporarily until she and Don were ready for children. By age twenty-six she had three children, and she knew Don would not hear of her working. When the children entered school, she began working on her college degree little by little. She finished only recently with the children now in their teens. "When I got married in the early 1960s," Ruth comments, "there was not as much choice as there is today. I stayed home and I was constantly delaying my own goals for the children or Don." She feels very torn now because her husband is so traditional that even with teenagers, he is angry about her own pursuits. Ruth projects they will eventually divorce. "I must have a chance to do some things I've always wanted to do, and now that my children are teenagers, I think I've earned that chance."

Ruth's case is not uncommon, especially among women who married in the 1950s and 1960s. There was little choice for women at that time. As adolescents, girls were counseled to marry what they wanted to be instead of pursuing the career themselves. They were conditioned, alas, expected, to live their lives through another person. That person, a man, was to be their reason for being. Girls believed in the marriage dream—a happy family, successful husband, doting wife and loving children. Only a man left the marriage dream when reality did not match expectation. Rarely did women leave a marriage. This is no longer true. Women are now as likely to ask for a divorce or leave a marriage as men.

The products of this period kept their emotions bound and hidden inside. Few women would admit to being unhappy or barely content. They thought that telling other people that the marriage dream was not working for them reflected poorly on them as women and wives. They thought others would believe them to be neurotic and, as a result, would not like them. After all, it was thought by many that a discontented woman had only herself to blame.

Women simply were not knowledgeable about their own self-awareness and their own needs. They were too involved in the traditions of the time to see objectively that they were constantly serving without satisfying their own unidentified needs. They were frustrated, restricted, tied down, and held back without knowing why. Films, television, and magazines stressed the romance which led to marriage and children. There were stories which revealed the lonely frustrated female in search of the right man.

Until efforts at consciousness-raising began, few women were able to recognize their feelings and acknowledge them as legitimate without consequential guilt.

Elaine had started graduate school and was feeling very guilty about leaving her two-year-old at home. Her husband called her during the day and reminded her that her child had cried when Elaine left that morning. He told her that the housekeeper's main entertainment was not the child but soap operas. Guilt built up in Elaine, and with her second pregancy she was a vulnerable target for being influenced to stay home. She quit school and filed away her books and papers which she had intended to use to write some short stories and articles. She spent her time telling "The Gingerbread Man" and "The Three Bears." She made block buildings over and over. She formed the habit of picking up items after every family member immediately, taking soiled laundry to the wash, and doing the chores nobody noticed which had to be done again and again. She kept doing these things by routine without any degree of satisfaction. She was trapped in frustration, easily depressed, and did not know why. She found herself gaining weight and becoming indifferent toward participating in social occasions. Elaine worried that she had nothing to contribute to a conversation except the latest in children's toys and the baby's new phrases, and so she felt awkward socially.

Conscientious mothers love their children and want to fulfill the needs of their children. However, unilateral efforts at motherhood leave voids in self-concept. A woman sees herself in relation to her children, not as an identity herself. She is Susie's mother and Bob's wife. Her selfhood is dependent on the whims of her child's temperament and health as well as those of her husband.

A mother who has chosen to stay at home rather than participate in the work force assumes many roles, and she does not always do so voluntarily. She becomes manager of the home and day-care center, organizer of everyone's needs, cook, chauffeur, personal maid, housekeeper, organizer of baby-sitting services, tutor, recreation director, home entertainment supervisor for her husband's business interests, and public relations specialist.

Women who trade in a job for motherhood can experience a sudden loss of identity. They are no longer in the secure position that once yielded them social acceptance in the work force. Some of these women find they are continuously having to justify to themselves or to others their decision to give up a promising career to stay at home.

Conflict:
Ambition and Tradition

Ellen had several strong influences on her while growing from girlhood to womanhood. She recalls early contradictions regarding the influence of her father who seemed to eliminate traditional role barriers early in her life before those role expectations became firmly entrenched in her mind. He told her that mathematics was easy, not the usual sort of comment made to girls by some less educated or unsuspecting parents who tell their daughters not to fret over numbers because girls are not made to be good in mathematics. Some have even been known to tell their daughters that the only figures girls need to worry about are their own measurements.

As a result of her father, Ellen grew up thinking about becoming an engineer or a meteorologist; she never thought any traditional male field was closed to her.

Ellen's mother was one who was "at home" for twenty years. She did not work until all the children were in college, and Ellen says that now her mother will admit how frustrated she was staying home during those years. Ellen was told by her mother that it was important to receive a college education, though she herself completed only high school. "A college degree is an insurance policy," Ellen heard, "in case something happens to your husband and you have to work." Her parents told Ellen she was the perfect daughter. She was eager to learn everything, to pursue knowledge in every direction, from mathematics to home economics. Her mother encouraged her as well, though she had stayed home to have babies.

Achievement was stressed in the family. Ellen soon found conflict between those achievement-related values and the life she saw in high school and college. She learned that the smartest girls are often disliked by the most popular boys; being smart she disregarded most of the teenage doldrums and went about organizing her activities as she chose. She was selected editor of the yearbook and class valedictorian. She was faced with the inevitable choices about her life. She was a straight A student, but society said, "You will get married and stay home and take care of your babies. You will use your mind through the home and the support you offer your husband."

Ellen also was affected as a teenager by an encounter with an adoring grandmother, whom she remembers to have been extremely upset when an older cousin, with a two-year-old child, went back to work. "It took me several years to get over that impression," Ellen recalls, "I thought my cousin had committed the sin of the century."

Ellen continued to achieve in school as was expected and she married between her junior and senior year in college. She had majored in mathematics, though she was not serious about the subject until a professor asked her to apply for a grant for her master's degree. "I laughed," said Ellen; "I couldn't believe it. I mean tradition and expectation really hit me between the eyes. I thought, 'Why do I need a master's degree?' If I had one I knew I would feel pressure to use it. It was time for me to teach math a couple of years and then have my expected babies." Yet Ellen's husband who was five years older than she served as her mentor and encouraged her to complete her master's degree. She did so while he served in the navy. She taught in a private school while he was developing his career as an industrial engineer. "Then I quit to have a baby and my life lost its shape. I left a job I loved; my brother was killed in an accident; my husband changed jobs with less immediate financial security but greater future potential. We moved from a neighborhood I loved into a house I hated. My adoring grandmother died. I felt like a zombie. I had no money, no clothes that fit, no babysitters, no relief, and then I realized I had no mental stimulation."

Ellen admits that that was the hardest time in her life and particularly in her marriage. She reflects on those times in retrospect. Her pediatrician told her that she must be happy in order for her child to be happy. This statement was a strong contradiction of her grandmother's words. These words about making a choice based on her own needs and prospect for happiness came from a professional, a man, during a time when women did not work except in a company town. Ellen recalls that when she tried to pick up a book to teach herself for mental stimulation the baby inevitably demanded her attention.

At that point, I felt anger toward my husband. I blamed him for getting me into what I felt was a mess. I felt an intolerable anger toward society for putting an acceptance on mothers who stayed home and a certain unacceptable attitude toward mothers who worked. I asked myself why I went to school to prepare to do menial things that required no training, such as scrubbing the toilet and the floor. About that time, the recession hit and I fould I could use economics to justify working with a baby at home. A babysitter, an older lady from down the street, suddenly popped into my life and I kept using her for years. I rationalized being gone because the baby would be napping and wouldn't miss me.

Before long Ellen found herself feeling angry about the housework, about working two jobs. She and her husband needed the extra money, and he began to help out around the house. He would wash the dishes and assume total responsibility for the baby on the weekend.

It was glorious to sleep on Saturday morning. It bothered me that there were some things he just would not do. He shared some of the housework and parenting responsibilities within limits. He might clean the bathtub all right, but in reality he never saw the dirt. The only way he ever learned to function around the house was by my going away to conventions. Of course, the house would still be dirty, but he did learn all the operational details of running a home.

As Ellen gained her professional pursuits, she began to begrudge the conflicts she had. She felt that her job in teaching mathematics and doing research was too demanding for her to be solely responsible for girl scouts, slumber parties, and birthday parties. Her husband had never even gotten a babysitter. The responsibility belonged to Ellen and the thinking and planning were all hers. She could never pick up and leave town because of all the preplanning that was expected of her.

It took a ten-year period for me to learn to cope. I went back to graduate school and earned my doctorate in mathematics. I was pregnant again, but this time, I didn't quit. I never again felt down. Oh, sure I had to struggle to balance a career and family but I never again felt that my life was out of control. I was angry that I could not achieve more, but when I got my doctorate I felt a tremendous mental and emotional growth. I felt some goals from within were being achieved. I got involved in so many things, I was being a super-

mom and superstudent and I was really trying to challenge my limits. My husband was proud and supportive of my efforts, which represented a change in him. We were communicating much more freely and openly than at any time in the past.

Unfortunately many women do not get the understanding and cooperative support that Ellen has attained. It is next to impossible for a working mother or a working father to give 100 percent to a job, and who wants to do that and keep a family? Realistically, if a person, male or female, gives 100 percent of his or her time to work, all other elements of life diminish. There is simply not enough time or energy left for additional pursuits.

A working mother must look at reality and make a choice. She must either do all she can to change her situation to a happy balance satisfactory to that particular set of circumstances, or she must accept the limits imposed by the additional demands she carries. To some women, the trade-off is worth the sacrifice. Ellen admitted that she knew she could not reach the heights of her profession because of her choice to give a large part of herself to her home, but she was emotionally prepared for that sacrifice. She knew herself well enough to understand her need for achievement and she found satisfying ways to meet that need on a part-time basis. She feels strongly that a person must be what she is and fulfill her potential and that pursuit can be accomplished through a realistic assessment of self and situation.

Accepting the limitations of a particular choice plays an important part in establishing a peaceful schedule, provided of course that those limitations are fair and equitable to a woman as a contributing member of a family.

Role definitions are limiting and binding. They require certain behaviors as a parent, an employee, or a woman. Continuous expectations for a particular role based on tradition or sex tend to restrict the freedom to develop and to be oneself. Roles that are imposed by others constrain women by building barriers around the choices women have to make. Responsibilities become dictates, not choices.

Laura knew that she wanted a career and a baby. A teacher with a graduate degree earned while working, she hoped to reach an administrative level in a large school system. She was well on her way toward achieving her goal when Laura and her husband decided to have a baby. The result was both rewarding and confusing.

I never dreamed that I would enjoy being a mother so much. I loved being pregnant but I was glad I had waited to have children. I was sure that today you don't have to choose between having a baby and having a career. When the baby was born everything changed. My mother cried when I told her I was going back to work.

"I can't believe it!" Laura's mother told her. "How can you leave this tiny baby?" Then Laura's mother-in-law came and she added to the mounting feelings of guilt. While holding the baby she said, "My poor baby, is your mother going to leave you? . . . all alone, you poor thing. . . ."

By this time soaring feelings had turned to strong emotions and Laura felt as if she were turning her new baby into an orphan. She felt that as a new mother she must be on the verge of child neglect. Guilt had brought with it doubts about her career goals which had previously been so clear. Indeed, her entire future now was clouded in a state of confusion.

It's one thing to say I'll go back to work immediately after the baby; it's another to actually leave my baby. What if my leaving does affect the baby in some way? I'd hate staying home for years, but I'm the baby's mother. I know no one can love my child like I do. My husband expects me to go back to work, but he doesn't understand how hard it is. No one else does. I've read all these stories about women who go right back to work and its sounds great, but it isn't that easy.

How can anyone be absolutely sure she had made the right decision in leaving her children to go to work—whether the children are infants or teenagers? The answer must be a personal one and it cannot be made by society, by tradition, or by well-meaning friends and relatives. It must be made in light of the unique set of circumstances and the needs of each individual. Certainly, a woman should not feel guilty of poor mothering because she wants a life of her own outside the responsibilities of motherhood. Welcome to the world of working mothers and the new age of freedom of choice without mandatory guilt. Times and circumstances are no longer what they were two hundred or even one hundred years ago, and the role of women must be reevaluated in the face of change.

Conflicts can be resolved through further understanding of the emotions behind the decision to give up a job. By relating these emotions to values and priorities, a woman can more fully enjoy the decision she has made. The satisfaction received by living out the choice can help fill the identity gap between professional woman and mother.

FILLING THE TIME

Some women at home equate their current job status to that of an on-call housekeeper. They fill time with tasks which may be unrelated to their purpose for giving up their career. They may lose the focus of their own right to satisfaction. The American housewife enters into the spirit of housekeeping through a compulsion to have her home "spic and span" and her children neat and happy at all times.

It would not be accurate to paint a portrait of an indolent class of American women who sit idly by while robot hands do their unbidden tasks; the work day of the American woman is, rather, subject to . . . the law that "work expands to fill the time allotted for it." As cleaning aids improved, standards of cleanliness have been upgraded far beyond the thresholds of sanitation necessary for health. With the new easy-to-use machinery, many jobs once relegated to others outside the home have returned to the home: the carpets which were sent out once a year to be cleaned or were beaten over the clotheslines in the spring now are washed every month with a machine devised expressly for that purpose; laundry often is washed daily because of the availability of washing machines and dryers, and this has made it possible for everyone to have a change of clothing, bedding, and linen more frequently. The list is endless and oppressive to the housewife. American women have engrossed themselves in housework and made their homes their career.[3]

There are, however, many other ways in which a woman at home may productively spend her time while bearing in mind her own emotions and her reasons for being there.

There are unlimited opportunities for filling the extra time at home productively. Gania had a baby and stayed home for a year with him when she decided to start her own company. She took an additional course to

[3] Cynthia Fuchs Epstein, *Woman's Place* (Berkeley: University of California Press, 1970), p. 105.

strengthen the skills she felt she needed for her new business. The company operated out of her home and was based on rewriting computer programs into a more understandable language. Started as a part-time venture, the business grew and Gania soon found herself in need of additional employees. Developed from an interest to keep her busy as she stayed home, the company was making increasing profits.

Not all women who wish to start their own business are this successful. However, many have found business opportunities develop from a talent or interest which can be largely done at home with little interference to the routines of childcare and with great rewards in self-satisfaction and fun. Many women write, design, paint, or sculpt, cater, or sew. The list of possibilities is limited solely by the energy and resourcefulness of the women involved.

Other women choose to hold a part-time job or volunteer position in their professional field in order to find continued stimulation, remain professionally active, and have time at home with a baby.

Sheri was highly trained in adolescent psychology but chose to give up her climb on the career ladder to stay at home with her two girls. She tried several opportunities to combine staying at home with part-time jobs. She found she could utilize some of her training productively by working with various youth groups, with community service groups, and in juvenile counseling. She is well satisfied, dividing her time and talents between volunteer work and her children. Sheri is not even interested in resuming her career.

Sheri remains happy to spend her time at home. The utilization of her training through her volunteer work keeps her chosen field of interest alive and renewed. Not only does she receive enjoyment from her choice to stay home and raise her children, but also she enriches that life by cultivating her mental capabilities and extending herself as she elects to pursue outside activities. Though she may not be formally "working," she is combining in essence her chosen career with her family, and she balances elements of both as do those mothers with "formal" jobs. In addition to the self-satisfaction she receives, Sheri is keeping herself up to date by using her professional skills and is feeling useful to herself and various groups with whom she works. Though she does not feel inclined to pursue her career in a formal manner, the activities in which she now spends her time are transferable into her career field as additional experience. In the future, Sheri will be prepared to resume her career if she changes her mind.

The Need for Flexibility

Plans do not always go as expected and some women find alterations are quickly in order. Charlotte, a thirty-two-year-old mother of a new baby took advantage of late motherhood and the career advancement she had achieved in her twenties. She had planned the child and did not want her job to interfere with the parenting of the new infant. Before giving birth, she was able to arrange part-time work suitable to her professional skills. This would have been impossible to do had she become a mother in her twenties when her skills were not as valuable and her professional expertise not as well known.

Charlotte experienced some new conflicts between motherhood and her work which were unexpected.

My job hours were really more frustrating than pleasurable. I felt such a bond to the baby which, being a first-time mother, I never expected. I actually didn't want to leave the baby even for a few hours. Things began to irritate me at work that I would have ignored the year before. I simply lost interest. I guess being a mother was more satisfying to me than anything else—especially when compared to the few rewards I was receiving at the office.

Some women try to work part time by converting what was once a full-time job into a half day. This arrangement usually will not work satisfactorily if the woman tries to squeeze the job of mother at home and the full responsibilities of a former job into one day or into one given week. If a full-time job is cut to part time, the responsibilities must also be cut proportionately.

It is difficult to manage time with a baby. The baby's schedule becomes the mother's schedule. The baby is the commander-in-chief of time. The mother's day is governed by baby food, baby laundry, and baby needs. The baby holds the reins of time, and the mother is the consumer.

Some mothers use this all-encompassing schedule as an excuse not to get anything done. Certainly there are days or weeks when the demands are heavier than others. There are also babies who are more demanding than others. But a few mothers find that a baby provides a good reason not to do something that they promised to do or something that they did not want to do. The baby then becomes a scapegoat.

Relax and Enjoy

In contrast, mothers who really are savoring every minute with their baby do not waste their time needlessly under the guise of full-time motherhood. It is not lost time to cuddle a baby for an additional hour if it gives pleasure to the mother and the child. Many mothers have difficulty relaxing enough to enjoy leisure moments with their child because they are thinking ahead of all the things which could absorb their time. They are unable to release the tensions of continuous responsibilities, not realizing that one of the rewards of being at home is the opportunity to forget about the clock and deadlines.

These moments are the ones that mothers with careers envy. These are the times that motivate women to abandon goals and to give in to total feelings of eternal motherhood.

Most authorities do agree on the importance of physical fondling and constant physical care for babies and small children. This is the one time in a child's life when continuous large-group care is not an acceptable technique for mothering. Institutionalized infants have shown clear effects manifested by mental, physical, or emotional disorders attributed to the lack of warmth and physical nurturing from an identifiable figure. (Some state laws forbid the licensing of day-care centers for the purpose of group care for infants.)

The fondling and cuddling of small children or the closeness of the mother to the other children at home is an important element of childcare. Mothers at home who spend periods of time away should be just as concerned as working mothers with the continuity of childcare. During the days of the extended family, when several generations lived nearby or under the same roof, there was always a familiar adult at home to care for the children when the mother was busy. However, families have become mobile and may be spread hundreds or thousands of miles apart. This may leave a mother with little help and may make relaxation and enjoyment more difficult for her.

In Mother's Absence

Educated mothers, whether or not they work, tend to place great significance on the environment in which their children live. They are concerned that their children are brought up in a place that is consistently warm and responsive to the children's needs for stimulation and development, that the environment provide the children with opportunities for creating and learning about themselves and their world. This ideal may be a combination of environments and may need to be planned carefully in order to accommodate some sets of requirements.

Time spent away from small children should be as carefully planned as the time spent with them. A woman may not be working at all or she may be working part time or working while the children are in school. She may be going to school or taking classes for self-improvement or toward a career goal. She may play bridge or tennis and participate in several interest groups. To accommodate these activities while being a full-time mother often involves a juggling act. Most mothers who choose to be at home instead of working full time in a career do so because they want their children to have the benefits of their presence and attention. To evoke separation anxiety beyond reason seems to go against the very purpose for staying home. This is not to say that children refuse to accept the mother's absence when they are attached to her and accustomed to her presence. The arrangements made for their care and the timing of the mother's absences will play critical factors in a child's acceptance of the situation. Playgroups, nursery schools, or provisions of care by a competent sitter whom the child enjoys will prove to be rewarding for the child and the mother. With proper arrangements, the child will not suffer because of time away from his or her mother; instead the situation may prove to be time well spent "recharging batteries" when both mother and child come back to their relationship with open arms. The situation to avoid during periods of substitute care is the hiring of inconsistent help.

For mothers at home who want to participate in outside activities several ideas from experienced mothers may assist in planning for time away.

1. Try to schedule club meetings, activities, classes, or part-time work to allow the maximum amount of contact with preschool children during waking hours. Avoid the development of insecurity by not leaving them consistently at nap time so they wake up and find you unexpectedly gone.

2. Select substitutes of yourself carefully. Allow children the opportunity to develop attachments before being left alone with sitters.

3. Devote exclusive time to the children for at least the immediate period of return. Once their immediate needs for affection wear off, they are again assured of mother's love and attention, and they will be satisfied.

4. Try not to get so involved in other activities that the children are overlooked. Some mothers mistakenly believe that because they do not work full-time jobs outside the home, their time at home is enough for their children. However, the way that time is spent and the exclusivity of periods for the children are ultimately important. Some mothers are so club-oriented or so heavily involved with volunteer work, tennis, bridge, or bowling that they forget their primary reason for being at home.

Claire was at home by choice. She had given up a nursing career when her daughter was born, and later with the addition of a son, she decided to remain at home permanently. Her husband's business career was doing well and so Claire did not need to work for financial reasons. She had the luxury of staying at home. At first, Claire was very attentive to the children's needs. She became involved in several civic and community clubs and suddenly felt very important. Since the children seemed to be doing well, she shifted her attention to her club and volunteer work. Before long, her clubs consumed most of every day, and about this time, she began to do heavy amounts of entertaining for Ted's business. Then she added traveling with Ted to her already packed schedule. At first they were gone for weekends, but they soon began to take extended trips. They hired sitters and a live-in housekeeper. The children began to have difficulty in school. Their grades were poor and they showed little motivation to do well. Socially, they were immature. Since their experiences of socialization were limited, they had few close friends. Claire bought them whatever they wanted to compensate for her time away. She hired a tutor to help the children with their homework because she was too busy with all her social obligations. "I really don't have time to attend all the minor details of the children's lives anymore." The children got progressively worse in attitude, maturity level, and academic achievement. Claire and Ted never woke up to the reality that they were neglecting their children even though she was an "at home" mother.

The working status of the mother has no effect on the attachment a child feels toward her. The mother's employment is not the crucial factor in whether or not she is close to her children. Most mothers agree that it is essential to devote enough time exclusively to their children when they are home.

Mothers at home often tend to forget this applies to them as well. They frequently equate being at home with spending time with the children. There are mothers at home all the time who virtually ignore their children. Unfortunately, some of these mothers are so tired after completing all their duties they are too exhausted to sit down and play, talk, or read with their children. Many of these mothers lack adult companionship, are preoccupied, or have other needs that go unmet. The result is a frustrated woman who cannot do her best in any role, whether it be mother, wife, or companion.

Some new mothers find the time so well spent that all thoughts of returning to work are abandoned. They realize that a part of them is given up in order to stay at home but they are willing to make the trade-off. The motive behind the decision is critical to their happiness. The reason must not only be positive but also reflect the freedom of thought in giving up a career for the new roles which will demand their time.

Margaret had never thought about leaving her job to stay at home. She worked throughout her pregnancy, and when the time came for the baby to be born, she took a three-month maternity leave. She saw what a different lifestyle a mother has. The flexibility was difficult to adapt to Margaret's strict routines. She found that she had to discipline herself to hold a steady routine, which she found to be more satisfying to her own needs. During her stay at home, she began to dread going back to work at the end of the three months. "I used to ask my friends at home what they did all day. Now I can see why they would resent such a ridiculous question, but I truly had no idea there was so much to do. And even more surprising to me was the satisfaction I received, which I never expected."

Before she stayed at home she could not imagine how her friends spent their entire days. After her experiences, she found that somehow the days were filled, sometimes in nice ways and sometimes in not-so-nice ways. It is the same as an outside job. On some days you enjoy the job and on some you would like to quit. But a mother at home always has the smiles and joys of her baby at her fingertips. Margaret decided not to go back to work. She realized that her days could be filled to her satisfaction. "I'll probably have to start at the bottom of the career ladder when I go back," she says, "but I made the choice. It was not inflicted upon me. The trade-off is worth it to me because I am hooked on my baby and motherhood."

Margaret, like many other talented and resourceful mothers, chose to give up her career, at least temporarily. The choice has nothing to do with self-sacrifice. It is a positive decision. Any sacrificial decision would eventually erupt with frustration because the choice was based on negative reasons rather than positive motivation. Mothers who make this decision to stay at home do so out of the desire to nurture. They enjoy taking care of their children. They consider this step to be a career in mothering, a refocus of their energies.

There are unlimited opportunities for filling the time when a former career woman makes the change from a structured workday to an unstructured day at home. She may need to provide her own structure in order to accomplish her series of tasks. Women at home need not feel pressured to live up to an ideal image or to maintain a rigid routine. Life at home is different from life in the office, and flexibility must be consistently and openly preserved in order to make the transition a happy one.

COMPARISON OF SELF
TO WORKING FRIENDS

The image of the "perfect woman" is more powerful than most women care to admit. The "perfect woman" manages to synchronize all aspects of her life. Her professional career compliments her personal life. Both yield high degrees of satisfaction. Many women strive toward this level of perfection. In reality, however, few ever come close. The image of the "perfect mother" further intensifies a woman's inner feelings. Women, especially high achievers, are vulnerable to conflict over the mythical images of both the perfect woman and perfect mother. Women can easily feel inadequate when they compare themselves to these images. In past endeavors they have always performed well. They have established patterns of perfection in their professional careers. As mothers, they want their performance to be just as perfect. They are not satisfied with anything less. They expect the home to be spotless and orderly at all times, the children to be perfectly groomed and well behaved, and the family routines to be smoothly organized. Alas, anything less reflects on their own inadequacy as mothers. And so they add pressure to their own lives by comparing themselves to this image of the perfect woman, perfect mother, the ideal mythical female. This is even more true for women who have established successful careers. They feel guilty about not being ideal successful women in every respect.

Women who may be highly qualified in certain fields have difficulty with the decision to stay at home even though they may possess strong instincts for the mothering role. These women compare themselves to their working friends in times of doubt, fatigue, or frustration, all common to mothers but especially to new mothers. Unlike women who have given up a job they did not really want, career women at home have a recognized need for creativity, self-expression, and challenge. They enjoy feeling productive and as a result feel good about themselves. This is food for the ego and positive reinforcement for improved self-esteem. If these outlets are suddenly removed the career woman, now mother, may experience feelings of withdrawal. She may begin to experience anxiety. She may find that she has unused mental energy as well. If these feelings begin to cause strain, there may be a negative impact on the marriage and her maternal role. A woman needs to feel satisfied about herself and what she does with her time and energy.

Professional women who set their careers temporarily aside in favor of motherhood meet with considerable criticism from their peers. These mothers find they are obliged to defend their decision again and again. There has been dramatic escalation in the societal and personal expectations of women since the women's movement began. The goal of having children and maintaining one's own career interests is no longer considered exceptional. Rather, it is now "allowable." Because of this, a woman at home may feel additional pressures from the professional world. She may feel the need to justify her decison to stay at home. Others may not agree that halting a career at a particular time is a wise decision. However, each woman should feel the freedom to choose the course she considers to be best for her life without pressures from others.

The women's movement has never said that all women should work or that all women with careers should continue in that direction. It has advocated the freedom of women to choose without the burdens of guilt. Women are entitled to make those decisions based on several criteria: individual needs (economic and psychological), personal goals and priorities, and family circumstances. Thus women should not feel the reverse side of "working mother's guilt" for deciding to stay at home.

Even though the traditional nuclear family is less common, some comparisons may still be made which create feelings of inadequacy. A traditional mother at home might compare herself unfavorably with the contemporary working mother. Many women who select the domestic life often resent those who choose careers. They may secretly resent the freedom or financial independence enjoyed by their counterparts in the labor force. They may envy the apparent glamor in the life of a professional woman with a responsible position. A career woman may be able to afford beautiful clothes and exotic vacations whereas the mother at home feels limited to jeans and shopping trips to the market. The working woman may appear to be more stimulating in her ability to converse as compared to a mother at home.

As a result of some of these emotions, a mother who has given up her career to stay at home may have hidden hostilities secretly directed toward the working woman. She may take advantage of opportunities without apparent cause to comment about one aspect of the working woman's life which is not as perfect as hers in comparison. This is especially true when women compare their children. Some "at home" women are sure that career women are neglecting their duties as mothers. These ideas and emotions may have emerged not from the imperfections of the working woman but from the mother's own need to justify her decision to stay at home. She wants not only to reassure herself that her time is well spent but also that those around her are convinced that she is very happy with her life choices.

Neither mothers nor child development specialists are objective about what is best for children. The choice is clearly dependent on a particular child, a particular situation, and the values of a particular set of parents. Comparing yourself and children to your working friends and their children is a common practice. Mothers want to be reassured that they are doing the best that can be done for their children. They continually maintain how much better off their children seem to be for the extra attention. They never fail to attribute problems that children of working friends experience to the employment of the mother. Anything that can be blamed on a mother's employment is usually done so by nonworking mothers. And it is a natural, though often unwelcome, occurrence. Mothers at home need to prove that they are spending their time well, that they are not wasting years of their life in vain. They are trying to prove that these years at home will be an investment which will pay off by leaps and bounds in the future years of their children's lives. In some cases they are right, but this belief cannot be generalized.

It is difficult to compare working and nonworking mothers because usually their job scope makes no difference to children. The differences lie in the traits possessed by each mother, what makes her the way she is. Some women who work have special talents or personalities which would benefit a child's development. However, some mothers who stay home have special talents and personalities too.

Disparagement of working mothers is not uncommon among mothers at home. Some even say that women work to compensate for their failure as mothers and wives. Though in a few cases this may be true, for most working mothers it is not. Some mothers who work, however, are happier than if they gave up their careers and stayed home. Consequently, this state of mind makes them better mothers than they would have been without working.

Mothers at home have several worries as they compare their lives to other mothers working. One benefit of working may be the shifting of parental roles, resulting in a lack of stereotyping by gender. Fathers seem to be less likely to share housework if the wife does not have an outside job. Thus the children may miss seeing the family run as a team.

Loss of Business Skills

Another concern mothers at home share focuses on their assertiveness. Some women are afraid that after five years of asserting themselves only to repair men and salesclerks, they would not be thick-skinned enough for the business world as their working colleagues seem to be.

There is pressure in some circles on women to be doing something productive. Merely being a mother at home does not seem to be enough to some women. A negative attitude is projected from "friends" who create pressure on those women who choose to stay home. They feel anxious about becoming stale or about limiting the bounds of their conversational ability.

There are some women at home who compare themselves unfavorably to their working friends for all these superficial reasons. In searching beyond the apparent, even though these mothers may be happy with their places at home, they are covetous of the working woman's success—the kind of success that is judged by the objective societal standards of monetary rewards. Women with professional success can have the luxury of choosing to work or not to work, while knowing all along they would not give up their careers. Many of the women at home never had any real choice because they were figuratively forced to quit since their salaries could not support a sitter for the children and leave enough pay to take home.

Contemporary women are, according to the media, talented and multidimensional. It is reasonable to assume that women of this stature should be capable of doing anything and everything they want to do. This includes the simple balancing act of manipulating a family and a career. Extreme feminist career orientation would rule out any alternatives. This does not eliminate the option for new mothers to stay at home and enjoy their babies. This extreme position would also affect mothers with older children or women with no children who want or need to stay at home. There is no need to justify this choice.

The emotional equilibrium for women is stretched by the pressures from peer groups or even from economic need. As a result a mother may lose part of her freedom to decide on her own, unconditionally, without comparing herself to her professional colleagues.

The emotions of motherhood change as children grow older. There is no justification for a woman to feel that she will lose out in the job market permanently if she takes a little time off. What is good for a woman and her child is what she feels comfortable about doing. The hows and whys of these decisions differ with every woman who makes them.

Some women feel that staying home communicates a stale professional life. They experience pressure because of their decision to give up a job to stay home. Other women who work in full-time careers experience similar conflicts. They may feel compelled to justify their decision to work. Society appears to have exchanged one set of guilt-producing myths for another. The nonworking mother may face as much guilt as the working mother. It becomes a no-win battle, and surely society does not intend motherhood to be seen as a battle. If this were the case, women would continue to live within a confining cycle of unrealistic expectations and inevitable disappointments.

There is a sense of failure underlying the lives of women because of a judgmental attitude in society. Both working mothers and mothers at home find themselves in a double bind. Each feels guilty, frustrated, and self-defensive. Each feels keenly different from other women and from other mothers because her situation and her philosophy are different.

One woman who founded her own company after her child was born described how she actually parted ways with a college friend in her community who chose to remain at home to raise a family.

"We were friends through our first children and had been friends throughout college and before. But as soon as I started to work, she began to sit in judgment of my life. In all honesty, I must confess I felt she was making a mistake to do nothing with her life except raise children. She didn't seem to realize how limited her existence had become." What this woman didn't seem to realize is the double-edged judgmentalism with which both women were striking each other.

There is no surprise in this comparison of one woman to another. The very terms which are used to define the position of women indicate judgment: "full-time" versus "working" mother. In reality, all mothers are full time. They do not surrender motherhood because they have jobs any more than a full-time mother surrenders motherhood when she is temporarily relieved of her childcare tasks. If this were not true, a full-time mother would cease to be one when her children were out of the house or enrolled in any school program under the care of someone else. Neither do mothers cease working because they stay home with their children.

Mothers remain mothers no matter how the semantics are slanted. They have similar emotions and concerns. They also share similar needs as women.

However, attitudes often lag behind realities, which represent the challenges of parenting and the frustrations as well. In trying to live with the traditions of yesterday we are not living with the changes of the present. By preserving past attitudes regarding women, no one can live comfortably with the present.

Comparisons of mothers at home to mothers who work is a common practice by both groups. Women have a need to justify their position. They also seek to communicate to society a decision appropriate for their set of circumstances. Each woman should decide on the basis of her own situation what is best for her. No one can decide for another. Whatever the choice, neither the woman who stays home nor the one who works should make negative judgments of the other. Women should be free of guilt in order to enjoy fully the benefits of their decisions.

LIVING WITH
YOUR CHOICES

In choosing to become a parent and to give up a career, both mother and father experience apprehensions about the way life will change. The simple relationships become complex with the addition of another human being. The camaraderie of friends, partners, or lovers shifts to co-parents beginning a life venture. Separate individuals, each with ideas, careers, and priorities, blend together as a family is formed.

Without children, there is not a great degree of stress about daily routines and chores. However, once a woman decides to give up her job or halt her career for a baby, there is a considerable amount of stress about each and every routine. The physical and psycholgical demands of childcare are enormous. For a new mother who has chosen to stay at home, there may be even more serious changes in her emotions as she suffers the loss of self, independence, and job.

New parents experience many conflicts in trying to perform their roles. They are trying to meet the needs of the child, and in the process, adult needs may be overlooked. The adult may have physical needs for rest which must be met. There may be a series of needs that the mother may have because of her decision to leave her work. She may need mental stimulation, a creative outlet, a challenge, more time spent with adults, a feeling of productivity, assurance of success. In short, a woman who makes the decision to have children and give up a job needs to know that her time away from what society terms "gainful employment" is being well directed. She needs assurance that she is doing what is best for her children, herself, and her family, for in order to be a well-adjusted mother, a woman must be happy with herself.

It is important for mothers who have given up a part of themselves to become full-time homemakers to find ways to balance their children's needs without sacrificing their own needs. A mother who is not a fulfilled person enjoying the fruits of her choices may in time suffer the loss of identity through the continuous sacrifices she makes. She may feel guilty and selfish about doing things for herself. Unfortunately, these deficiencies will build and eventually surface in problems: emotional, physical, or mental.

When women must bear all the burdens of parenthood alone (contrary to current trends of shared parenting), they are actually increasing their independence. If they are receiving none of the critical support from a husband necessary for sound mental and physical well-being, why then is there need for a partner? When family roles are polarized there is an increased sense of separateness rather than unity.

One of the signs of a healthy relationship is that it can adapt to change. Realistically, there may be some resistance during the period of transition, but a major change will affect the family as a system, not just the one who undergoes the change.

Changes occur as various members of the family grow older, pass through predictable life stages, or pass through periods of developmental stages. Some change is voluntary; some is not. Some changes are more noticeable than others. Some changes are more complex than anticipated (such as having a child). When change occurs, as it inevitably does in life, the family will feel the impact. One member of the family may resist change, but in many cases it will only delay or cause the situation to be more difficult, thus increasing anxieties and conflicts. The result can be damaging to a relationship as well.

Staying home does not force women to be maternal. Mothers who prefer being at work will not do the best job in the mothering role. They are staying home against their will and will be consequently unhappy about it. Those full-time homemakers, however, who prefer the maternal role will usually do a good job provided they did not assume that role because of social pressures. A forced acceptance of the maternal role is a disservice to the child, who may be better off in the care of others while the mother works. An "at home" mother must be satisfied in her position in order to transfer that satisfaction into the duties she performs.

The mother's personality, stamina, and emotional stability will also influence the relationship with her children. The schedule she maintains and the needs of her children are important factors in that there must be some correlation between schedule and energy level. A mother can do only as much as her own capabilities will allow. To take on more will only bring additional conflicts, pressures, and frustrations which do not add to the happiness of the mother or the well-being of her children.

There is no doubt about it: Having a baby around is different from any other time in life. There is no comparison of the continuous needs of an infant to any other developmental period in life. Mothers who choose to stay home out of deep sensitivity toward an infant may be more self-confident and less fearful in handling and caring for their babies than working mothers or mothers who are at home because of outside pressures rather than personal choice. These "naturally" affectionate mothers may be fortunate in being able to stay at home. Certainly there are many women of this nature who must work by necessity and are unable to enjoy the extra time spent playing with their babies. Usually this type of mother is more tolerant of irritating behavior and interested in every detail of her baby's behavior, no matter how minor.

The absence of support relevant to a working woman's life can stop her career advancement at any time. At every turning point the woman is faced with crucial decisions about whether or not she should work. Strong conflicts are evoked by tradition, norms, or attitudes which pull women in many directions and disguise the clarity of decision making.

Motherhood has traditionally been a mystic, exalted state. It has inspired songs, stories, prayer, sculpture, paintings, and embroidered pillows. Women aspired to become mothers just as men wanted to become soldiers. Each sex has its ultimate responsibility. Terms such as *Mother*

Nature and *Mother Earth* connote the power and sacrament of motherhood.

In the past a woman who had not borne a child before her thirtieth birthday was considered barren. She was a figure of pity. She was frequently asked to explain why she had not had children. Motherhood and careers were considered to be mutually exclusive. Career women were commonly referred to as old maids because they had to work rather than respond to the natural call of women, that of motherhood.

Motherhood no longer possesses the same degree of mysticism or exalted position. It has been discussed, analyzed, debated, and studied. However, motherhood is not a science, nor is it an art. It is a choice for a particular way of life.

Being a mother is no excuse for being less than a woman can be–for developing less than her human potential. A woman is a person who builds her life through choices. She is a planner, a dreamer, a builder. She builds an image of herself as worthy of the respect of others. She builds an opportunity to change attitudes about other women from her example. A woman builds hope for the future as she teaches her own daughters and sons how to ungender the mothering process. She teaches them early that parenting is a choice not an obligation. She teaches her daughter that she can aspire to be a fire*man* if she chooses or she can be Bat*man* on Halloween if she chooses.

Understanding the demands of motherhood, the possible trade-offs and consequences to a career, and the emotional conflicts surrounding the sudden changes in life can help a woman formulate her rationale for this extremely important series of decisions.

A decision to give up the job is more socially acceptable than almost any set of arrangements which have been made to balance work and home. However, a woman must be sure that the decision is made with extensive knowledge about what to expect. This preparation can deflate the impact of the emotional conflicts inherent in a major life decision.

IV
CAREER
AND FAMILY

6

The Decision: Combining Both Worlds

MANY WOMEN have been trying to combine a professional career and a family life for years. In the process, they have encountered conflict in their struggle to balance home, marriage, children, and work. Situations that have generated the emotional strife inherent in the conflict have occurred both at home and at the office.

At home, a women can anticipate possible collisions with her husband and children. Her husband may resent her earnings or job promotion. He may not be able to accept her career goals or success. He may expect her to give up her job if he receives a job transfer. The children may have schedules which clash with her career demands. A woman may discover that she does not have time for routine household chores. This may trigger unpleasant controversies. She may eventually conclude that her career is restricted.

Because of family responsibilities, a woman may have to reject job assignments, out-of-town trips, promotions, or transfers. Women who combine both worlds experience obstacles that can block future professional and personal growth. Being aware of potential obstacles can ease the conflict when it occurs. Women can then be more optimistic about the chances of successfully combining both worlds.

ROLE CONFLICTS

Changes in lifestyles in family living patterns often occur in a family in which both the husband and wife have careers. Inherent in these changes are predictable difficulties which can be the source of family conflicts.

The time management of daily routines frequently appears impossible. Without joint cooperative effort from both the husband and wife, schedules are not kept and tasks are not accomplished. Men who are suddenly faced with actively participating in activites such as babysitting, dinner preparation, laundry or cleaning house sometimes find adaptation difficult. The working mother often feels frustrated if the husband doesn't participate in these chores. The standard stereotyped division of labor with home chores is impractical when both partners work. Conflicts are minimized if each person shares the responsibilities of childcare, meal preparation, and household chores.

The "best laid plans" are still susceptible to last-minute crises. When the babysitter does not show or a child comes down with a sudden illness, someone has to stay at home. Is it the husband or the wife? Parents have the option to take turns in these situations or place the responsibility on one of them, as has been the custom in the past.

Childcare duties are still assigned as a part of a mother's role, and thus in most families, it is the wife who deals with these matters from established custom to present day.

Many career women are discontented in their home situation because they are expected to shoulder all the responsibility for the care of the children.

Kathy, who is a buyer for a department store, expressed her feelings of frustration with childcare duties. She must travel to New York three or four times a year. She also must be away from home for other job responsibilities. When she is out of town, even overnight, the household routine seems to fall apart. The children's daily schedule is usually disrupted. Eating and sleeping routines are changed. Her husband takes them out to eat rather than cooking at home. He seldom has them in bed at their usual time. The children may miss planned appointments. She feels that she has the major responsibilities for the children not only when she is at home but also when she is away on business trips.

Although office work may be a priority, children still have to eat and have clean clothes for the next day. Occasionally the controversial issue of "who does what" emerges, especially when both parents have excessive career demands at the same time. Regardless, someone has to prepare the meals for the children and supervise preparation for bed and for the following day. In many situations, a compromise is the only practical answer, but the majority of households are not open to such changes in family roles.

Common weekly household chores can interfere with the career schedules of both parents. With the logistics involved in just keeping up with the complex daily routines and career responsibilities, who has the time to go to the grocery store, the bank, or even fill the car with gasoline? Worse yet, who has time to take the children shopping for new shoes or new clothes? These recurring obligations do not have to turn into conflicts if parents are prepared to deal with them.

Role conflict can occur for many reasons. Some women experience role conflict because they do not see themselves as mothers and professionals. Some of these women have difficulty seeing themselves as mothers at all.

> *Conflicts in women's roles stem in large part from the isolation of the family. No longer integrally imbedded in the community, the family has become specialized in the related tasks of managing feelings and bringing up children. As "guardians of the home," women are still expected to specialize in kitchen and kindergarten, homemaking, and childrearing, tasks which contrast sharply with the cognitive, achievement oriented, and independent world of work and public life. Trained and often motivated for working life as well, they are forced to suppress, sublimate, and displace their desires for "fulfillment".[1]*

A professor was quite dismayed at her reactions to her infant. She was very uneasy around the child. In her office, the tell-tale signs of motherhood were absent. There were no photos, drawings, or notes. She stated that such signs meant to her that women could not accept themselves as total professionals. This professor, however, began to mellow as her child grew older, visited her office, and wanted to leave his remembrances. She still reflects on her feelings of motherhood as lacking in the intuitiveness she thought came from just being a woman. "I was not a

---

[1] Kenneth Keniston, *The Uncommitted* (New York: Harcourt Brace Jovanovich, Inc., 1965), pp. 294-95.

natural mother," she said. As a result, her inner conflicts about her new role became more and more apparent. She was not able to resolve easily her frustrations, but she managed to do so with the gradual help of her family and a loving housekeeper who took over most of the maternal role. Just being a woman does not guarantee natural maternal instincts.such deficiencies can be resolved with the willingness to meet them and work out the conflicts.

Personal Conflicts

Family conflicts that are less obvious center around the relationship that the working parents have with their children. The children do not always understand why both parents work. The child may interpret a parent's absence from the home to be a form of rejection. The child may wonder if the parents want to spent time with him or her. A child will usually welcome an explanation of why both parents work. If the child is told what his parents do while at work, he may feel more integrated into that other world. With a basic foundation of understanding, a child will react to scheduling conflicts in a more rational manner. When neither parent attends the child's open house at school or parent-teachers day, he or she may be consoled somewhat by knowing the reasons for their absence. Communication is vital with working parents and their children. Enhanced understanding on the part of the children is an important factor in resolving conflicts which occur. Emotional support is a major source of conflict in dual career families. Individuals, because of their own needs, are often limited in the support they can extend to each other. The demands of their career may require a very supportive person. Traditionally, the supportive person has been the wife. The working wife, in return, has no one to turn to for the same need of fulfillment unless her husband can reverse his role. This balance of support is difficult to achieve. Both partners have to be willing to be the support figure to the other person. Women are just beginning to learn the importance of a supportive partner.

The complexity and at times the upheaval associated with office politics can create the need for a great deal of home support. A woman can supplement her knowledge of office politics and gamesmanship from her husband, providing he has had more experience with the "old boy network." A woman should receive support and understanding at home when the office is involved in power struggles or political strife. A partner has a golden opportunity to act as mentor to his wife; to teach the intricate struggles of an office. Most men have been involved in these battles previously. For women this is a new dimension of work, and understanding the functioning of office politics is another way in which a supportive husband can assist his career wife and lessen the possibility of role conflicts at home.

A husband can also help his wife when he encourages her to progress professionally. He can show enthusiasm for her success as well as her attempts to achieve success. In essence, he could become an additional source of strength.

Women who do not have the emotional support of their partners struggle with inner conflict. Such was the case with Delores. At thirty-six, she had worked in an office for ten years. She chose to work on her master's degree to pursue more specialized training. The university she attended was almost one hundred miles from her town. Since it was such a distance, she remained there during the week. Her husband was non-supportive of her desire to go back to school. He wanted his wife to be at home to take care of him. He did not look past his own physical and immediate needs to the consideration of her career goals. When he called her at school he told her that his shirts were dirty and unironed. He did not perceive her work as a career. She was just working at a job. He placed little value on her emotional needs for support, let alone her decision to progress in a career.

Professional Conflicts

A woman is often confused with a man's perspective of a career and a job. Most men grow up knowing that they would work and be involved in a career. They do not always identify a woman's work as her career. Women add to this confusion. A substantial number of women were brought up to be wives and mothers. These women grew up wondering if they would ever work at all. They saw work as a job, not an ongoing career.

Women have conflicting views from men concerning personal and professional career goals. Men usually see the personal and professional career goals in one. Women see them separately. Because of this difference, men have instinctively placed less value on a woman's career. The definition and knowledge of the value of a woman's career can help to avert conflicts and set a foundation of basic understanding between the two people.

Salaries are often a source of conflict in dual career couples. Some men have difficulty accepting the fact that some women earn more money than men. Status and career value are largely dependent on earning power. The person who brings home the higher salary is the head of the household or holds the true breadwinner position. Degrees, honors, accomplishments, and titles do not mean as much as the actual dollar amount on the paycheck. Women who are in higher management levels risk the onset of conflict if they advance to higher paying positions.

Dorothy and Drew have experienced emotional turmoil since Dorothy's last promotion. She has been in editorial positions for fifteen years and has risen step by step up the career ladder. Because of her hard work, she has received several promotions. Drew owns an independent business. His business is successful and he and Dorothy could comfortably live on his salary alone. He has accepted her career and has encouraged her successes. But he never dreamed that she would have risen so high in her profession. Drew feels less masculine when he picks up the checkbook and looks at the deposits Dorothy makes from her paycheck. Drew insists that Dorothy not tell anyone the amount of her salary.

Another problem in working families which can cause conflicts between husband and wife is the concept of "her earnings." Society has placed a lesser value on the wife's paycheck than on the husband's. Banks and government agencies have reinforced this idea that her paycheck doesn't count as much as his. Young married couples are often advised to "live off his income and bank hers."

Couples themselves carry out and encourage this idea in the way they deal with paying the bills, their checking and savings accounts, extra expenses, relaxation and emergency funds. Some partners will have the "important" bills, such as the mortgage and car payments, made out of his paycheck and the lesser household bills coming from hers.

Some couples are essentially living independently, although they share a house and the marriage license. They maintain separate bank accounts to handle their money. The money never is jointly shared nor distributed, like the "his and hers" bathroom towels—not to be touched by the other person. Traditionally in this arrangement his checking account maintains the greater cash flow and thus is seen as more important.

Job promotions can create a crisis for the family with both parents working. What otherwise would be a happy occasion turns into a predicament with seemingly no workable solution. If one partner is jealous of the other's success, a promotion can aggravate and intensify those feelings.

When the husband is offered a promotion which involves moving to another city, the wife's career may be harmed. She has been expected to make that sacrifice in the past. Men do not ordinarily accept the reverse of this custom. Most are unwilling to even hear of moving because of a wife's job. One person's career frequently suffers when a move is made that benefits only one of the partners. The career advances of one person can handicap the career opportunities of the other.

Bob's job requires a transfer every two or three years. Heidi is a dietary consultant with the city's hospital. Although she is highly trained and skilled, her field is somewhat saturated and jobs are at a premium. Heidi landed the present position after six months of intensive job searching. Before the couple married, Bob wanted a guarantee from her that she would move if he received a promotional transfer. He also knew that he wanted to marry a career-oriented woman. He failed to realize that the two often clash. Career women are hindered if the husband's job is continually in flux. Heidi stated that she feels as if the period of transferring is temporary. She said, "The transfers are not easy; it's not an easy time. I have felt totally fragmented. But, a strong facet of our relationship is that we can compromise. We both have learned how to compromise." In essence, Heidi has traded off future career development or advancement for the lack of role conflicts with her new husband.

At times, the separate careers of the couple take each of the individuals to different cities. When this happens much stress can result. The conflicts that arise with the separation can cause irreparable damage to the relationship. Couples who experience separation anxieties usually have to come to terms with their feelings. One couple agreed on a realistic decision to live in one city in order to prevent the conflict from continually recurring and causing deterioration of their relationship.

Other times, limited numbers of available positions can produce conflicts with couples who are in the same field. They often realize that they are competing for the same positions. A realistic option is for one of them to go into a more specialized aspect of the field that requires further educational training.

Social and Career Demands

Couples who have excessive career demands can discover that their social life is less than adequate. Because of work obligations they may repeatedly have to cancel planned time with friends. Energy levels can also be a source of conflict. If one partner is completely exhausted and the other is ready to go out and have a lively time, disagreements can result. Time that should be spent together in actuality produces more stress and significantly affects not only the individual's energy level but also the desire to share events. Finding time to relax is a difficult task. Couples have expressed the difficulties involved in, first, finding the time to relax, and second, having the energy to enjoy it.

Other role conflicts become evident in a couple's social life. When a woman is well known to other people, her husband may feel over-shadowed by her. Unless he is secure himself, conflicts will most assuredly develop.

When husbands and wives are in the same field, role conflict is again likely to occur. One couple, both attorneys, experienced an emotional conflict because she had been asked to join a more prestigious law firm than her husband. Socially, the situation was magnified and both felt somewhat awkward. To avoid stress, a partner should have enough self-confidence to be able to share in the joy of the other's achieve-ments. Each must be a stable and secure individual in order to avoid competition.

Many men have difficulty handling the idea of a successful wife in the same field. Some are basically fearful of being overshadowed and em-barrassed, appearing less competent than a "female," and (worst of all) becoming the focus of teasing and jokes from "the guys." This fear is, in itself, role conflict with a working wife. Some men manifest this com-petitive fear by requesting a more impressive title for their own job or by trying to persuade a wife to enter another field altogether.

A part of the insecurity many men experience is based on a fear of losing a woman because of her success in comparison to his. Men are not accustomed to competing with women, especially their own wives. In the final analysis, she may be far more skilled than he; yet by custom, she should have submitted her talents for his use.

Other role conflict occurs when men and women are in traditionally opposite fields. The husband of a female politician has especially awkward moments on receiving invitations marked "spouse" or "candidate's wife." Such invitations may ask him to teas, fashion shows, or rap sessions on "how to be a political asset to your husband." Very few men have suc-cessfully learned to handle such predicaments, but it is a ripe field for educating men to do what women have done for centuries. Husbands of women who have been elected and appointed to government office experience role conflict in varying degrees. Some of these husbands have even asked their wives to resign their posts because they could not accept her position in comparison to his.

Families that have remained together without severe conflict sometimes seem to be a minority. In some of these cases, careers of husbands and wives have kept pace with each other and they have managed to resolve conflicts. Some have successfully shared the same profession and have developed a common ground in understanding problems that each partner faces. Couples who have managed to remain close and have separate careers have found it important to support each other and to be proud of each other's accomplishments. They have learned to cope with role conflict in their marriage.

CAREER RESTRICTIONS

Women who work outside the home often encounter restrictions to their careers. These restrictions are the result of conflicts that occur when a woman has a family and also a career. Her time is limited. She does not have extra hours to spend at the office. She has other responsibilities at home that need her attention. Because of demands at home, she may purposely refuse a promotion, especially one in which a move would be required. School vacations and the holidays present a babysitting dilemma. She sees herself perpetually making choices between the advancement of her career and the daily maintenance of her home life. Out of a practical necessity, she usually chooses to care for the needs at home, those of her children, over choices that could be beneficial to her career. Working mothers continuously experience the time squeeze. When five o'clock arrives, they have the responsibility to either pick their children up from the day-care center or meet the babysitter at the front door. Women with children in school feel conflict about not being home when school is over. When mothers are unable to leave work early or find a job that ends early in the day, they encounter problems with after-school sitters or day care. Women who have small children or children in elementary school often choose careers or jobs that enable them to be home when their children get home from school. This is why so many women in the past have chosen to work part time or in jobs that coincide with school hours; their role as a mother was not interrupted or threatened.

There are obvious career limitations in terms of salary and advancement opportunities.

Some women purposefully choose career combinations that will give them the opportunity to be away from the children and give them the emotional satisfaction of working outside the home. An important consideration for these mothers is the flexibility they need to meet their children's schedules. Teaching is one profession that allows a woman professional stimulation but has hours and vacations that are the same as their children. Jobs that require evening meetings or "on call" responsibilities often produce stressful situations for a mother. These women usually can survive in this type of job if they have "on call" babysitters or a live-in housekeeper. Most jobs that have hours convenient with children's school hours are those which are typically considered "female positions." These are in fields which are heavily populated by women. As a result, most of the jobs are lower paying and have little chance for advancement. Many are, in reality, dead-end positions. Women exchange promising careers for jobs that tie in with family life. Jobs such as teaching, library work, and nursing can be adapted to a family schedule and create fewer conflicts and stress by disrupting home life. These professions also have fewer opportunities built into the system for future advancement. Women have become increasingly aware of the conflicts inherent in career trade-offs.

Some women do not look forward to promotional offers. Although they realize that they are skilled and have excellent performance records, home demands are such that promotions would have to be declined. New job requirements usually include travel and long hours. Some women realize the conflict of those responsibilities and make the choice to place their career second as long as their children are young. They also have realized that unfortunate restrictions are placed on future promotions.

At times the career restrictions of women have been self-imposed. Many of these actions stem from the childhood experience of dependency training and role modeling. Their formal education frequently was devoted to "female occupations." Their tendencies were to choose limiting careers that would be convenient to marriage and motherhood. Many women felt compelled to enter these female-oriented careers despite the recognition of their own interests and talents in other fields.

Women who have ventured away from traditional work expectations have endured many conflicts. A woman may have launched a career in a field that is unsympathetic and unwilling to allow employment for a working mother.

Performance of job tasks within certain time frames are a predictable element of many demanding careers. A woman who is in a managerial position faces time pressures every day. These women must rely on well-developed plans for their children. They cannot afford to miss a work deadline, a business meeting, or a chance to progress in management by demonstrating irresponsible actions. Women in similar positions discover the key to survival is a flexible, adaptable home schedule with alternative plans in the event of an emergency. In this way, the woman can still fulfill her work obligations and keep up with responsibilities at home.

Career-oriented women are continuously met with conflicting situations. A mother may have to miss her child's Christmas party because of a job commitment. Children may not be able to participate in after-school team sports or extracurricular activities because their mothers cannot pick them up or take them to the required practices. School holidays can be a time of stress. The school-age children are home alone and usually bored. As a result they may call their mother at the office four or five times a day.

Although work can be fulfilling, rewarding, and satisfying, it can also be emotionally and physically draining. After a difficult day at the office a working mother is still expected to go home and take the major responsibilities for cooking, cleaning, and care of the children. She may feel depleted of her energy by the end of the day. When her children and husband want her attention she may have no energy left to extend to them.

Because of the monumental effort required to balance home and career some women have chosen to refuse promising career opportunities. Other women have dealt with each conflict as it arises and tried to reach a point of equilibrium that is satisfactory for them and for family members.

Women who want both a career and a family should understand the difficult road that lies ahead. With advanced awareness, planning, and support, women are discovering that they can have successful careers. Occasionally, however, a woman's choices place restrictions on her career. As long as women have the major burden of responsibility for the home and childcare, women will continue to decline career opportunities and, in essence, side track promising careers. Thus, women as a talented resource will go undeveloped unless the load of "women's work" is shifted according to the changes seen in each situation.

DEALING WITH SUCCESS

"There are certainly no Harvard Business School cases on how to deal with this," Peter Bernstein quoted Mary Cunningham in his article "Upheaval at Bendix" in *Fortune*.[2] Mary Cunningham was too successful. She rose in her company too fast. Defaming gossip spread that tied her advancement with an alleged sexual relationship with her boss. The fact that she was bright, knowledgeable, skillful, and received her master's degree from the Harvard Business School was overlooked. A man's rapid advancement in a similar situation would more than likely be admired, not maliciously denounced, as was the case with Mary Cunningham. Women who go beyond traditional expectations, especially in top management, are often met with unscrupulous gossip. Their advancements are not always seen as the just reward for hard work and ability. Rather, promotions are unjustly perceived as a result of romantic involvements or favors, as if no woman could possibly achieve on her own merits.

Success complicates life. Success for a career woman further intensifies inner struggles of emotional conflict. Women have not inherently been geared toward success. Women have not been taught how to deal with the pains of success. During childhood years, a female was considered successful if she won a popularity or beauty contest. From early years, males are encouraged to be successful through achievement and accomplished tasks. As adults, men continue to compare their success with their achievements and they continue to strive. Women, on the other hand, have often been made to feel guilty for their achievements in careers traditionally controlled by men. Now, however, fewer men and women comment that such women take jobs away from men.

Avoidance and Concealment

Some women have dealt with success through avoidance behavior. They stop short of their career goals or refuse promotions. These women

[2] Peter W. Bernstein, "Upheaval at Bendix," *Fortune*, Vol. 102, No. 9 (November 3, 1980), p. 56.

purposely keep themselves from advancements or recognition in order to avoid threatening someone else. Other women use avoidance in less obvious ways. They accept the promotion but through their actions make themselves look inadequate and unable to perform the job. These women passively, and at times unconsciously, arrange a stumbling block in their career path.

Many women have dealt with success or the possibility of success by simply avoiding it and at times sabotaging their professional careers. "Topping out" is a form of career sabotage. Some women on the rise deliberately derail their careers. This can occur by removing themselves for two or three years from the job or by leaving the job because of demands and hours. In this situation, a woman avoids dealing with the difficulties of the career instead of solving the problems. Other examples of topping out are turning down good opportunities or promotions and quitting a job when the realization is made that an ideal job does not exist.

For years, women tried to conceal their accomplishments and hide evidence of their success. They have done so to protect the insecure nature of others. Some women protect their husband's delicate ego by disparaging or toning down their own work accomplishments. They build up and at times exaggerate actions of their husbands. They make such comments as "He earns more than I do"; "He has a higher position in management than I do"; and "His job is more important than mine." Women have also dealt with their own success by denying their own accomplishments. Rather than take credit for their hard-earned labors, they instead attribute their success to luck or to accidental reasons. "I just happened to be at the right place at the right time," is a common denial of one's achievements. Some women, who are in reality very skillful and deserving of recognition, continually utter self-demeaning remarks. They make a point to tell others not to be too impressed with their job or title. They also belittle their level of expertise and quality of performance. The woman who is continually putting down her own success is many times assuming that her actions will shelter another from feelings of inferiority.

There are men who do feel inferior and who are threatened by a woman's achievements. These men usually possess traditional views of women. They probably grew up believing that they should be the most important person in a relationship. They believe they must be the boss. They believe that a woman should not be competing for the same job that a man has. These men frequently identify with the social image of a man and his masculinity. They feel that they must have the power and control and have a career more significant than any woman. They often refuse to take pride in the accomplishments of a woman. When a man like this has to interact professionally with a female, he tends to separate the female from her career position. He deals first with the fact that she is a woman, and second with her professional training, skills, and position. Men who are threatened by career women are usually trying to hide their own feelings of insecurity. They no longer have it made just because they are men. They are beginning to realize they have to justify their existence and importance on their actual performance and achievement, not on their masculinity alone.

Successful women have had to bear stiff penalties for their success. High-achieving women repeatedly have to defend their accomplishments. Often, they also encounter jealous reactions from peers, friends, relatives, and co-workers. As a result, they may discover that others are questioning and attacking their desire to succeed. In essence, others criticize the ambitious feelings which motivate career action.

Ambition

Many women are chastized and discouraged from ambition. Traditionally, ambition has a negative connotation for a woman. Women are not supposed to be ambitious. In reality, however, many women are ambitious. Women want to succeed and reach their goals just as men have always been expected and allowed to do.

Women themselves had a difficult time accepting the term *ambitious* as a characteristic of their gender. In the past, ambition was a term used to describe the working quality of man. Women have been conditioned while growing up not to be professional or successful. This was a male role function. Women have in turn feared a loss of femininity when associated with the term ambitious.

Women have been conditioned to separate their female status from job and career aspirations. As a result, inner conflicts have been built into this framework. With this reasoning, a woman has to choose between career success and feminine identification. A man, however, never has to struggle with this dilemma, as his personal success is many times the source of his professional success. Traditionally, this has not been so for women. Professional and personal goals were separate, and usually brought conflicting choices. Women are just beginning to realize that they no longer have to choose between a career and being a female. They can be feminine and still have a career.

Another conflict inherent with a woman's identification is between professional ambitions and personal childcare responsibilities. Women often find themselves asking questions such as "Can I have a commitment to both my children and my career at the same time?" Decisions that are beneficial to a woman's career goals are sometimes not in the best interests of her children or family. A move or change in jobs may cause disruption to the adjusted patterns of living in the family. Women ask if they can be satisfied in both worlds as a mother and a professional. Feelings of guilt can at times outweight pleasures of success. A woman finds that she has less time with her children and husband and changes occur in her marriage and close friendships. An editor returned home from a business trip and was met at the door by her four-year-old daughter, who said, "Mommy, mommy, I thought you were never coming home." This statement took her by surprise. When her husband travels for his job, the children do not appear to be upset. However, the idea of a woman being away from her family for business reasons is begrudged by her husband and children.

Women can deal with ambition by first identifying that they do have a strong desire to succeed in their career. As a woman internalizes the concept that ambition is part of professional success, they are less likely to be afraid of their own feelings. Women who are ambitious tend to be self-assured, independent, assertive, and able to make decisions. Professional ambition simply means a desire to get ahead in one's career. In order to get ahead in a career, women should identify their career direction, clarify goals, build self-confidence, separate their strengths and weaknesses, be able to take new risks, build network systems, and build systems that support. Getting ahead in a career usually means making a deep commitment to the career.

Joan, thirty-six, is an architect with a small firm. Her boss, who is also the owner of the firm, had a meeting with her on her third-year anniversary. He offered her a promotion and an opportunity to become part owner in the business. He told her one of the main reasons for this action was because she was so ambitious and he valued that quality. Joan had never before thought of herself as ambitious. Rather than be overjoyed with the promotion and opportunity she was slightly unnerved with the idea of being ambitious.

There have always been successful women involved in work outside the home. The numbers, however, were quite small. Today more women are in the work force and more women are in management and administrative positions. Thus, the conflicts that come with success are involving a great many women rather than just a limited few.

PRESSURES OF SUCCESS

Success usually brings change. The change can be positive or negative. Even positive change can bring new stress in relationships with others. As a woman's career moves upward, she is increasingly involved in her work. She enters a new way of life with new pressures, goals, commitments, and responsibilities.

A developing career takes lots of time and energy. While a woman is putting forth effort into her career, loved ones often feel confused. They sense feelings of both happiness and resentment. The combination of both positive and negative feelings can lead to strained relationships. Suddenly a woman finds herself in the position of being too busy to relax with other people. She often finds herself alone.

When two people are in separate careers they seldom experience the same career stages simultaneously. This is often a source for strained relations. While one person is expanding and developing his or her career, the other may be at his or her peak. A situation such as this can produce stress. Both individuals have their own set of needs at their own career level. Dual career couples often meet with conflicting goals.

Success is usually physically and emotionally draining. A woman can experience an inner struggle as a result of depressed energy levels. She can find herself resenting the demands and expectations others place on her. Relationships can begin to distintegrate. A woman can find herself in a conflict of time and energy between her career commitment and the needs of friends and loved ones. Business commitments or required deadlines can necessitate the cancellation of a social invitation. Friends may interpret this as a personal rejection of friendship or love rather than a time squeeze caused by excessive career demands.

Success can produce pressure and stress because of the lack of time. A female can find that she has no social life and has little time to spend with friends. She is frequently declining or cancelling social invitations. Friends who do not understand usually pull away. They can become angry and very hurt by a successful female. To help alleviate stress caused by time pressures, the female can start by organizing her time and being open and honest with her friends about her conflicts.

Successful women commonly receive double messages from others. Friends and relatives react in a variety of ways. They show pleasure, anger, jealousy, pride, criticism, and support. Women may feel that their success is ruining their marriage or their friendships. They no longer have time to spend with their friends, and not uncommonly, this is interpreted incorrectly as rejection. Both friendship and marriages are often strained when a woman experiences success.

The combination of a successful career with close friendships or marriage can require a great deal of understanding and patience. Relationships, however, can withstand the stress of a commitment if based on love and trust.

Women want professional growth and success. They also want close friendships, honest relationships, and love in their marriage. Women can help themselves by realizing that possible conflicts in work are inherent with success. They should be alert for the danger signs in relationships. A successful female should accept the fact that relationships will change because of changes in her life. New career demands and deadlines will at times take priority in her life.

Success, however, has a positive side also. The rewards of accomplishments can be shared with friends and relatives. Women can discover that the conflicts inherent in success are manageable. A woman can actually combine both worlds with increased understanding and happiness.

7

The Decision: Coordinating Conflicts

WOMEN WHO HAVE MADE the choice to combine a career and a family have experienced difficulty in coordinating the many conflicts. Only an independent, highly spirited maverick would consider having both at the same time because of the resources needed to accomplish the feat successfully. A woman attempting such responsibilities was doing so against negative odds. In the past, a woman who made that choice knew what a struggle she was facing.

Working mothers are still fighting an uphill battle. They are knowledgeable and assertive and gaining in strength and power. They rarely return to the nest unaffected after working in the competitive labor market where they must prove themselves twice as capable as men in order to earn half the salary.

Women are more aware of their position and potential power than at any time in history. They know how to speak out and how to exert influence. As women have gone into the world and become leaders, they have changed. In turn, the credibility of women as leaders has been enhanced.

Pioneer women who learned to lobby and demand the vote have served as strong role models for their able descendants. Women have become strong political forces. They have seen the need for change in policy and have learned to organize and run for office in order to implement that change. Women have learned how policies are made and how to become the policy makers.

In the past, men were expected to deal with all extraordinary situations whether temporary or long term. This honor was not bestowed because of presumed magical power or supreme innate ability. Rather, additional responsibilities were assumed by men because they had an active and dependable support system at home. A man had a readily available wife at home who could step in and fill whatever voids were left. Women have rarely had the benefit of a supportive partner at home.

Every decision is compounded by restricting details which women must work out, unlike their male counterparts. Inequities of this nature are common and often unrecognized by male and female alike. The freedom which women are allowed to enjoy is impeded by such unfair practices. Yet this pattern frequently continues to be perpetuated by women who assume the added responsibilities and burdens without question. The tradition is also perpetuated by men and women who do not recognize that these burdens are imposed on women.

The working mother who obtains personal satisfaction from employment may not have excessive guilt if she has adequate household arrangements. She is likely to perform as well or better than the non-working mother. The satisfactory combination of all the elements necessary for a smooth balance of career and family is difficult to achieve.

There are many impediments to satisfactory arrangements for career mothers. Some involve logistics, routines, schedules, and obligations. Other hindering factors are social or psychological in nature.

Guilt is a very strong emotion with which almost all working mothers must deal. At times, guilt can logically be rationalized and eliminated. However, few working mothers have been able to handle guilt without the pain of emotional stress.

Other conflicts may occur which combine the psychological stress of working with social and physical limitations inherent in the functions of a working mother. Few women can count on the man of the house to be the man *in* the house. Although more husbands are learning role reversal and cooperative family living which support a working mother, few share equally in parenting and housework.

After working a full-time job, the average working wife puts in at least six hours of housework and childcare compared to one hour and a half for the average husband. The male privilege is ingrained into boys by adoring, serving mothers. These fathers who sit back and watch their wives work are setting examples for their sons and daughters. While these boys are growing into adult males, they are learning to "use" women and to be served by them. Manipulation can be learned at an early age. Boys learn that the career of a woman is "extra," secondary to their father's career, certainly not to be taken seriously.

As a result of continuing attitudes negative to working mothers, little support is given to help overburdened women who work either by choice or necessity. Mothers are left feeling guilty, doubtful, and restricted. These feelings drain both their physical and mental energy. Such stress can cause a working mother to be less productive in her work, which might otherwise be mutually beneficial to her and her family. A high degree of satisfaction in a job or career can provide strong positive feelings of independence and self-esteem which transfer beneficially into the family situation.

GETTING ORGANIZED

Not all working mothers can compare to the television stereotypes of the sexy superwoman. These women are seen as organized, always in control, and amazingly never tired or sweaty. Not many mothers can identify with the television women who waltzes in the kitchen door with her tennis trophy in hand after an obviously easy win (every hair is still in place). She is presented with a cake baked by her handsome husband who is at home awaiting her arrival. The woman who sings a happy tune about doing the laundry, feeding the kids, getting dressed, passing out kisses, and getting to work by five of nine is hardly typical. She delivers a convincing advertisement for the eight-hour perfume for the twenty-four-hour woman. Yet how believable is she in reality? We have all seen the television mother in designer clothes who waxes the floor to a glowing shine. As a tireless temptress, she sexily removes her rubber cleaning gloves for a night motivated by that special fragrance which will drive her companion wild.

How can the average woman compare to these glamorous twenty-four-hour-a-day working mothers? Most would more readily identify with the forever dieting woman who cannot talk too well because of her sinus, stuffy head, and cough. Yet she assures us that her husband is "taking care of her." Of course we never get a glimpse of this wonderful man, the prince on the white horse, but we fantasize that he does exist.

Some women are only eighteen-hour-a-day workers. A few actually get to sleep from midnight to sunrise before struggling through another marathon day.

Many days are filled with anxiety. Too many things are scheduled, which means pressure mounts as the activities of the day settle into their order of priority. As activities seem to run together, a woman may question her decision to combine a career and a family. Coming home to a messy kitchen and whining children after a day at work can produce conflict. A woman may wonder what happened to the promising lure of self-satisfaction, independence, and productivity.

Most working mothers have learned the importance of a schedule as one way to relieve the potential for conflict. One case of split-second timing is illustrated by Terri, who promptly bolts from bed every weekday morning at 5:45 A.M. At age thirty-eight, Terri has planned each minute of every day. She has no time for perfume or kisses, not with three children, dirty laundry, lunches to pack, and breakfast to make. Terri says that her daughter at age nine will soon be able to help out more.

But the boys, she reports, are growing up just like their father— expecting it all from me. And the worse part is, I don't know how to stop the cycle. I've built up so much resentment from having to be responsible for everything, it seemed to me, while my husband Ted just had his job. Sure he brought home more money than me, but that's just the point, how can I justify his working at home when my salary doesn't measure up to his? Is it fair?

I finally exploded in midweek once last fall. I had to work before I go to work, work while at work, and then work after I work. I'm no superwoman, that's for sure. But I got to the point where I said "Hey, I'm doing total maintenance for every person in this house." I'm being squeezed to death physically and emotionally. Yet I enjoy my work in research and God knows we need the money.

After my outrage, Ted agreed to help with some of the housework and he even gave the boys additional chores. It's working out better although I still can't find any time left for me. Ted puts the children to bed and sorts the laundry or occasionally "cleans" the kitchen (I use that term loosely).

Some of the problems working mothers experience invoke getting organized. Some mothers feel a well-planned schedule preserves order in their day. Other mothers find they can plan only one day or one week in advance. Like anyone else in the working world, mothers must occasionally work late or irregular hours to meet deadlines. All the well-devised plans can completely change at a moment's notice. Women learn quickly that flexibility and alternative planning are very important. A working mother who is trying to organize around her schedule and maintain all her children's needs will find she is bearing an unrealistic burden whether she is married or single.

Marian is a working mother. Her job entails juggling the roles of wife of a medical doctor, mother of two daughters, and state representative of 25,000 residents in a Southwestern city. She is also a political activist and campaigner. She relates that men throughout history have always reported pressure to beat the clock. "This usually is not associated with women," Marian said, "but a busy working mother must have time-saving techniques. I am a big list maker. I make a note of everything and then I can prioritize my time. If I have a great many items on my list, I'll go through and mark them in importance A, B, or C. Then I can organize the A's in order of importance and leave the B's and C's until next week or next month." Marian has learned through her organizational talents not to procrastinate, but she does not feel obsessed with getting everything on her list accomplished. Learning to use little bits of time, Marian squeezes the most out of ten or fifteen minutes during the day. She uses the telephone a great deal for shopping, and ordering items for the children to avoid walking around shopping centers. Initially, Marian balanced career and home without outside help, but eventually as she saw the need for a more flexible schedule because of campaign commitments and meetings, she hired a housekeeper to live in. Her husband, being a doctor, could not provide the back-up system needed for the daughters since he was on call at a nearby hospital. Marian also had the help of her parents, who were able to step in as needed with the children or with campaign arrangements.

Frana is a working mother who buys time with appliances such as food processors and freezers. She is a plan-ahead cook who bakes and freezes in large quantities. There are always enough meals in the freezer for several days ahead. In addition, if she cooks only on Monday, then her other days are free for girl scouts, shopping, cleaning, or her own choice of leisure activities.

Establishing a daily routine is a time-management approach many mothers use successfully.

Occasionally children have regularly scheduled events which can be planned ahead, such as music lessons, tennis lessons, practices and sports activities, or church events. More difficult in planning are the sudden needs which are brought to a mother's attention with all the force and immediate need of an erupting volcano. Many children, especially teenagers, are skillful in parental manipulation. They know exactly how to approach a mother to get her to attend to their needs. The teenager's crises usually involve earth-shaking events such as a birthday party (which absolutely cannot be missed), a skating party ("I'll be the only one not going, Mom"), or a club meeting ("they can't meet without me.") Children learn tricks and combative techniques to win decisive battles: crying, pleading, trading, and arranging to win over traditional parental techniques as logic, reasoning, awareness, and sensitivity to the needs of others (particularly mother). Some children become so adroit that they are actually making their mother feel guilty for "leaving them" to work or for "neglecting them" instead of making herself available on a twenty-four-hour basis as a chauffeur. Many of these skills can be transferred to later life. Children who become experts at this kind of manipulation can grow up to become opportunists who use others to achieve their goals.

Some women suffer more problems than others in their efforts to combine a family and a career. Women who have had a hard time getting back to work because of lack of support or lack of organization tend to experience more conflicts than those who step easily out of one organized world into another. For those working mothers whose conflicts continue, problems seem to breed more problems. Some of these women have difficulty shedding the problems of their children or home at any time, especially when their energies should be directed toward productive output. However, some women never seem to get their lives fully organized or get their priorities in order no matter which direction they choose.

COOPERATIVE
HOME MANAGEMENT

Men have always been reluctant to share the burden of housework. Household chores have been designated as women's work. Overworked wives are more common than not, and those wives who manage full-time jobs in addition to housework have much less free time than male companions. The dissatisfaction arising from too many responsibilities may have been a contributing cause of runaway wives and mothers, a trend of the later 1970s.

Getting housework done is usually low in the list of priorities for working mothers. Most regard housework as something that has to be done which gives little satisfaction in itself. However, everyone enjoys the satisfaction of a clean house. An orderly house promotes feelings of relaxation on arrival home from work. The pattern of housekeeping in the lives of working parents is one which results from attitudes about housework, compromises, and priorities. Whether a family keeps its house neat and orderly or cluttered and disorganized is an issue that depends on the needs and level of adjustment of family members.

Women of later generations, inspired by feminist literature, have come to regard housework as a family affair. They feel the same responsibility for taking care of their own homes as women of previous generations, but they are now more likely to insist on an equitable sharing of the burden of housework and the care of the children between men and women.

Men who marry career women may find themselves having to sink or swim in regard to household responsibilities. Some busy professional men whose business lives are tense and competitive enjoy the satisfaction of simple tasks at home. Some of them have learned new hobbies, like cooking or refinishing furniture. They have uncovered talents they did not know existed. Men who are willing to participate in cooperative home management find that managing a house and family together can pull a family much closer than the isolated task differentiation assigned by tradition. Some men may want to assist in family chores or learn to cook and their wives simply will not let them. Some women do not want to relinquish their roles or settle for less than the level of satisfactory performance which they perceive themselves as able to render. Women may feel that they have to keep their hand of inspection on all work that is done. They still manage to keep on top of the work by providing praise when praise is called for and corrections when appropriate. This is a time-consuming and draining habit that is unnecessary.

Some contemporary couples see housekeeping as a part of their relationship. Reassignment of roles is a frequent part of getting things done. Every mother should have household help, and the people who should help are the ones who make the mess.

Hiring a Headache

Hiring outside help is one alternative for working mothers who cannot find relief by sharing responsibilities. Those who can afford domestic help may find it to be as much of a headache as a help. Billie, an accountant with four boys, said she needed the help to keep the house in semi-orderly condition when the boys were young.

I have since taught the boys to accept responsibility for household duties and it has helped them learn independence. They'll always be dependent on someone if they don't know how to manage the details of their lives. So I crossed the lines of tradition and taught them things they at first called "sissy."

When they were very young, I must have gone through half a dozen cleaning ladies a year. At first I was unaccustomed to dealing with hired help. I think I actually catered to them because I was so ineffective in saying what I expected and then drawing the line for performance. They seem to sense that with four boys, they had the advantage. Some of the women I had were unbelievable. In addition to eating all the food in the house, using my perfume, and taking one coffee break after another, some didn't show up at all. Or another worked so slowly and accomplished so little, she wasn't worth the money I paid her. One woman went through all the family belongings and discussed details of her other employers.

My final attempt at household help came when Robbie was in kindergarten. An older woman came to work and brought her grown daughter with her. They worked as a team and in half a day, they were finished and gone. This seemed to work great and for close to a year I felt fortunate. I did have to make a list of everything that was to be done, and I mean everything. If it wasn't on the list Ruby wouldn't do it. Eventually Ruby starting bringing her husband. For several months I was not home when they cleaned but I assumed everything was the same. I was angered when I saw him go through my house and out to the car where he retired to drink. Both of them had been smoking and dropping ashes on my carpets and furniture, although they had been told not to smoke in the house because of Robbie's allergy problems. I have since given up on hiring headaches.

Benefits of Routine Management

The routines involved in housework do not have to be a burden, but to run smoothly a house must be managed as a cooperative venture. No woman should have to bear the entire burden alone. Even if she enjoyed the distraction of the routines or derived some satisfaction from doing housework, the role model she presents to her children serves to perpetuate the myth of women as functionaries. The possibility is lost for broadening the attitude of the family and restricting the unifying bond a family feels as each member makes contributions for the benefit of all.

There are as many possibilities for cooperative home management as there are families. Some prefer rotating duties on a daily, weekly, or monthly basis. Others prefer continuous responsibilities in one area or "taking turns." Different lifestyles may open various possibilities for contributing to the general welfare of the family. Some larger families have found monthly "sign-ups" work well. Still others manage time and learn cooperation through color-coded systems in the laundry, wherein each family member has his or her own colored receptacle for clean clothes. The person who sorts clothes from the dryer can separate into various colored baskets which each family member is responsible for picking up, unloading, and returning to the laundry area.

Inherent in developing a joint home management system is the learning which can be derived from it. Cooperation is a vital tool in the adult world as well as the world of children. The earlier this becomes a part of the nature of children, the more likely it will become a rooted element of their character. Certainly transfer of cooperation into the business world and society in general is a positive goal which can be achieved through the constant need to demonstrate cooperation in living together.

Attitude is another area of learning which can be a result of cooperative ventures at home. Not only do children and spouses have the opportunity to expand their attitudes about women's roles, but they can also help eliminate the narrow attitudes still in existence through the examples they set.

Responsibility and independence are traits most mothers want their children to learn. However, these characteristics are not learned solely in the classroom. Children spend more of life at home than in school. The examples they see as well as the opportunities they have to apply responsibility and independence are the factors which assist in their learning.

DINNER MADNESS
AND EQUAL RIGHTS
ON THE HOME FRONT

A time of turmoil for the mother who has put in a full day on the job is the dinner hour. Five to eight in the evening seems to be a time of common madness in organizing, preparing, and shifting gears. For some mothers the shift to a domestic routine is more difficult than for others.

Factors which complicate dinner madness are more than one child at home anxious to obtain their mother's attention, a job that is strenuous or tense which makes a woman (or a man either) feel physically exhausted, an unorganized household where no one else has helped with supportive chores, or an unpredictable situation at home which prevents advance planning and preparation. The shift from professional responsibilities to parental responsibilities is not automatic. It takes time—time to unwind and rethink. Without this period of adjustment, residues of tension more than likely will be transferred to children or husband. Small irritations grow into monstrous dilemmas because they have grown from an infestation unresolved, perhaps unrelated to the issue at hand. From this kind of tense situation, the issue easily becomes a bomb and suddenly, to the surprise of everyone, the blame for the entire dilemma rests on the working mother. The mother may feel tense from her day at work. But fathers often feel tense too, and they are never scorned for it or made to feel guilty for bringing tension home. Excuses are made for men who come home tired and irritable waiting to be soothed in their castles by a wife and loving children. Is a woman not entitled to the same right in her own home?

Women are even asked to believe that their reason for existence is to be there when a man returns home from work. She is to stand at the door wearing baby doll pajamas, his slippers in hand and his dinner on the table. Some adults, male or female, would enjoy being pampered in such a manner, but a mature adult relationship is not so one-sided. In terms of basic needs for love and attention, women and men are not that different. They both deserve equal consideration for their needs and desires. One partner should not be given greater attention because that is expected. Partners in a relationship give to each other as the need arises and not in a one-sided routine manner.

Many couples feel the woman is responsible for dinner preparation and childcare during the hours of madness because a woman is usually home before the man even if by thirty minutes. This is simply unfair punishment for working hours. Women who try to arrange their schedule in order to arrive home early to coincide with their children's arrival are not rewarded for this valiant effort. They should use this time to shift gears and enjoy the children. Instead a working mother is expected to go straight home, and as soon as she hits the door, she is to begin preparation for the evening meal. After dinner and clean-up, a working mother is exhausted.

This need not be the case. Some couples decide that during the child-rearing years, they will both try to get home early from their jobs. They are willing to make professional compromises: to schedule days for one or the other to be home early or for special activities with the children; to go to work earlier in order to come home earlier; to arrange after-work meetings or breakfast meetings; to bring work home.

Getting home on time is one compromise working mothers and fathers need to make no matter how old the children are. Unfortunately, this insistence on normal or flexible work schedules is contrary to the stereotype of the ambitious, hard-working American trying to climb the ladder of success. However, a trend seems to be building that time should be given to children by fathers and mothers and that those of either sex who ignore that need may eventually find themselves with problems or no family at all.

GETTING SUPPORT

The traditional basic assumptions about the roles of husband and wife and father and mother are slow to change. The family lifestyle may not correlate with tradition, but the role expectations may remain the same. Daily lives may involve dramatic shifts in responsibilities while expected roles lag behind.

When a wife and mother is away from home as often as the husband and father, conflicts are bound to surface if expectations do not change with life changes. Routines in the home cannot realistically be carried on as before. Both husband and wife are tired at the end of the day, and both face children with a need for attention from parents.

Nevertheless, the management of the home and children is still seen as primarily the job of the mother. She may be working as hard in her job as her husband, but he perceives this job as additional responsibility for her. He may view her job as secondary to her job at home. Even the woman may feel emotional conflict because of the old roles carried into a contemporary culture. Role models, or examples, set by mothers of husbands with this type of attitude helped to mold these feelings and expectations about the role and duties of the wife and mother. This attitude, coupled with childhood and adolescent fantasies from textbooks, media, and life, directly affect developing minds concerning marriage and family roles.

Compromises needed for contemporary living are not determined by any rule book. There has been no accepted guide to help couples adjust to changing roles. Thus women have continued to struggle to maintain two jobs.

Some skeptics continue to advocate the old traditions, and they ignore the misfit of old roles in a changing society. These skeptics have sought to impose their school of thought on women through guilt by threatening the end of the American family, the neglect of children, or the decline of successful marriages. This type of attitude has only managed to hurt women more and is not substantiated by conclusive research.

Part of the solution to the perpetuation of assumptions that women are responsible for dual roles lies in the training that men and women receive for their roles as parents in earlier years. They are impressed early in life with what the roles and responsibilities of the mother are supposed to be. Until these closed attitudes are challenged by open-minded mothers and fathers, children will continue to act out what they learned and saw in their childhood years.

Much of the "expert" advice passed along to women have come primarily from male sources. These male pediatricians, psychiatrists, and psychologists may have been sympathetic to mothers and their problems, but they simply did not know what to say to a mother who insisted she could be a mother and a career woman at the same time. As a result, these "experts" emphasized the traditional nuclear family and the need for maternal presence. What happened to paternal presence in this great advice in previous years? Father was excused for working by males who were also working.

Elizabeth had always worked. Halting her career long enough to deliver babies and pamper herself with luxuries for the first few months of her babies' lives, Elizabeth thought in terms of her career and family combined. Her husband was not the thorn in her side in this issue. It was her doctor. He continually commented about her "too active life," stating that she should "settle down more." Since he had so many years of experience, as he often reminded her, she would be well off to listen to his advice and stay in the kitchen for the children and the bedroom for her husband. Elizabeth considered her doctor a kind, older man and did not relish the idea of a confrontation with him. As a result, she usually listened to him while her blood boiled inside. She resented the feelings he made her have, yet she respected his ability as her doctor enough to put up with his "personality quirks" as she called them. "The problem is," she reflected,

"I think he failed with his own children and that's why he lectures others. Maybe failure made him an expert, but I'm not pursuing the road he traveled. My children are well adjusted and our communication is open as they reach the teenage years. I don't foresee any drastic changes down the road. They are happy that I enjoy my work and so am I."

Some husbands feel that their role instinctively requires them to be dignified. Such a sophisticated image insidiously described a fellow for whom others relinquish their own needs in favor of his. Women whose husbands fit this description usually repress their own needs consistently for his needs as well as those of the children. These women are in need of more support than husbands and doctors give. They are faced with the real world of work, expectations of a boss, financial obligations, and unmet personal needs. When does this woman's need take precedence over her husband's and her doctor's?

As life partners, many husbands seem exceedingly adept in maintaining ignorance of their wives' real needs. A wife who chooses to work is doing so because of the satisfaction she derives from professional pursuits. A wife who works out of necessity is doing so because of the needs of her family. Whatever the case, the home routines continue, and husbands who take no interest in supporting their wives are missing the opportunity to be a real partner and helpmate to their life companion. A few husbands, when asked, would say they helped out in the household. However, their definition of "helping out" is not in accordance with that of their wives. The wives of these men might say they did nothing. Some of these husbands think that just being a nice guy is enough. Maybe for some women it is, but not for most.

Psychologically, the need for support is as crucial as the help in physical labor, and yet for some women this support is more difficult to accept. It is difficult for women to shift their personal expectations about their role as wife and mother and to actually transfer responsibility to the male. The household has always been the woman's job, and as a matter of attitude and perspective, women think in terms of home management— though these management skills are seldom carried over into the business world. The perpetuation of limitations of this nature are damaging to women, to their self-concept as well as to their perceptions by others. Women must be willing to let go, to let the male take responsibility for tasks that were formerly hers even if it means that her standards of performance are not kept.

Sue, one of these women, at age forty-one had worked most of her life. Her career was interrupted briefly for childbearing and she continued to stay at home for the first two years of her children's lives. She was anxious to resume her career and felt that her children, seventeen and eighteen, have profited in many ways from her work.

> *When I was struggling to combine my career and family, the women's movement was not as strong as it is today. For years, I just never expected my husband, Michael, to do anything, except occasional baby-sitting. I mean, I really felt the duties around the house were mine, and so while he relaxed in front of the television on Saturday or went to a ball game with his friends, I stayed home to clean the house or to plan meals for the family for the coming week. I never thought about asking him to share in those duties. I expected to do it when I got married because my mother had done the same thing. Now I realize I have helped to perpetuate the myth by my own example and I've talked to my son and daughter about changing their attitudes when they marry. I hope it's not too late for them even though they didn't see a very good model for change in their own mother and father.*
>
> *I went straight home from work every night and prepared the meal alone while my children did schoolwork and my husband watched television. Oh, he sometimes puttered in the yard. I don't blame him at all because I knew that even when I wanted to ask for help, it would be more work for me than just doing it all myself. You see, Michael has never been taught how to do any of the household chores. I doubt that he knows how to vacuum and dust, and I'm such a per-fectionist about missing spots or fingerprints. I know the room is clean when I do it, but if I left it up to him I would only have to do it over.*

Passing Along the Myth

Generations of women have felt similarly and yet have not taught men, as husbands or sons, how to perform these tasks satisfactorily. First, a woman must be willing to let go—to delegate to the male a set of responsibilities. Then she must support his attempts to perform them. This means she must refrain from continuously pointing out the negative aspects of his performance and focus on the positive. If it really bothers a woman that there is dust behind a chair, she can learn to wait until he is not around and quietly clean it to her satisfaction.

Women now must be aware of the opportunities for training their own sons. Let them learn to wash their clothes as well as make up their beds. Again the myth is passed on to sons by mothers who step in and clean up their rooms or pick up their clothes and justify their actions by saying, "That's the way boys are" or (even worse) "He's just like his father." These same mothers show double standards to daughters if they have girls, and both sexes note a difference and harbor the thought as they grow into adults.

Like Sue, some women have never questioned the traditional family arrangement. They have continued to raise their children while holding down a full-time job. Now, with hindsight, the women's movement and changing times allow women to structure their lives within optional frameworks.

Rhea was unprepared for motherhood when it came. She was finishing a graduate program in a mostly male class in business management at a prestigious Northeastern university. Her husband had completed the program and was just beginning to climb up the career ladder. He was not in a position to help out with a baby because his job flexibility was an important element to his career.

The only support he could give was verbal. It was a terrible time to have a baby but I was told that I probably couldn't have children, so I felt like it might be now or never. Ben and I agreed that this was what he wanted but the major sacrifice was mine. I really hated dropping out of school. My professors seemed to enjoy the "too bad you won't make it" comments. They thought I wasn't really serious about my profession although they never questioned any of the male students.

I was determined to keep going but I had to be careful because of some problems with the pregnancy. Besides, how many executives in major corporations would take me seriously looking like an elephant, glowing with motherhood and apple pie? So, I kept up my studies on my own and after Rich was born I wanted to resume my program of studies. However, Ben was traveling some and we just couldn't find good help. I stayed home another year and then I got the best source of support possible. We moved my mother from Ohio and any trade-offs on our privacy were well worth the comfort of having her there to help with Rich. When I first went back to school, I was crushed to hear my baby say "Mommy" and to reach out for me when I had to leave. But, I was relieved to know that my baby's grandmother was there to give him the kind of warmth and cuddling he needed. That kind of support and reassurance is invaluable.

Factors Affecting Support Needs

Diane, a thirty-two-year-old dress designer, gave up her professional pursuits in her first marriage to be at home with her husband and child. When she was divorced, she went back to dress designing and found she was constantly called to New York. It was not unusual for her to be away from her child for a month. Diane found this to be very guilt producing because she had no support for herself or her daughter. She loved her child and she loved her life but she was torn between career and child. She decided her priorities had to be set and naturally these would reflect the direction her career would take. Instead of living in frustration, she decided to give up her hopes for greatness and concentrate on her child. She narrowed her career by designing a single line of dresses rather than a multiline.

Decisions and sacrifices similar to those made by the dress designer are faced by many women. Without the support of husband, relatives, or friends a working mother will usually find a difficult and frustrating situation. Managing a career and family without help is an insurmountable feat, but there are some women strong enough to accomplish the impossible.

Decisions which must be made by a working mother involve several factors. These variables should be examined in order to arrive at a realistic assessment of the situation. Some of the factors which weigh heavily in making decisions include the amount of support the working mother can actually depend on, the degree of travel and job responsibilities, and the particular needs of the child or children involved. A woman who travels infrequently would have little or no conflict from that factor in her career and family decisions. If her child was insecure and was in need of large amounts of attention, the decision would be somewhat more complex. However, if she had a steady and flexible source of support from a mother or a husband, her career conflicts would be reduced. She need not worry about a consistent figure to care for her child during her absence. Decisions which must be made by a working mother are never easy, but sorting out the variables which are the potential causes of conflict can help clarify the direction of those decisions. After grouping the variables, a working mother must be prepared to weigh each one according to impact and importance.

Conflict increases for a mother whose job demands or family requirements are substantial. Adding to the complexity of the situation may be
the lack of support in caring for the child or the need for help at odd
hours. This type of working situation will involve continuous conflict
because the variables are at odds with each other. There is no way to
balance the variables without changing the weight of one of the factors
involved. Either the work hours must be stabilized, the support system
must be adjusted, or the needs of the child must be met more easily. For
a working mother who is faced with such an unbalanced situation, the
picture is grim. A woman who is under continual stress cannot function
productively or be a normal and happy individual while successfully attending the responsibilities of motherhood. This is difficult enough for a
well-adjusted, happy mother who tries to deal with the imbalance of
scheduled demands and the needs of work and family. For the working
mother to achieve success in all areas of endeavor is almost impossible
without the degree of support which a man expects and usually receives
from his wife. Though much needed, wives are not allowed for the working woman and she frequently must add this role to the list of responsibilities which she already administers.

Men usually manage to make a marriage contribute to their success
and prestige. Most married women do not receive the same proportions of
professional support.

> *The man's status set [i.e., marriage] is complementary and reinforc-
> ing and the woman's is not. The professional woman who marries and
> permits proliferation of her family statuses must early face the fact
> that she has no wife at home.*[1]

Resentment toward the working wife is expressed in many ways.
Many husbands are not willing to sacrifice any of their accustomed conveniences even though the work may bring satisfaction to the wife and
additional money to the family. This type of attitude, which engenders
resentment toward the wife and begrudges her personal development, is
selfish. Some of these husbands may be in favor of their wives working but
they do not expect to change their routine in any way. They expect their
wives to have dinner on the table, the house clean, and slippers at the door
by the time they arrive home. They object to the time and energy their

---

[1] Cynthia Fuchs Epstein, *Woman's Place* (Berkeley: University of California
Press, 1970), p. 101.

wives must spend on the job, and they are usually unwilling to support their wives by helping with meals, babysitting, or laundry. They have a feeling of omnipotence; the man's job should take priority over the woman's, and the wife should be the only one to make adjustments.

Women who are married to difficult or nonsupportive husbands experience extra emotional and physical burdens. Anything which arises in the household is blamed on the wife's employment. Subtle efforts are made continuously to make the wife's tasks more difficult. There is usually dissatisfaction in the relationship which stems from the lack of willingness to compromise. The result is often frustration and a sharp division of companionship. Many divorced women were once married to men who refused to give them the needed support. The difficulties of a marital arrangement of this nature cannot be blamed on a wife's working. The obstacles can only be traced to selfishness and an attitude that makes a poor foundation for a marriage of two people who need to grow as individuals and to rely on each other for support.

A totally opposite experience is much more in keeping with contemporary attitudes which match the changing times.

Paula had worked throughout her twenties, and she became a mother for the first time at thirty.

It was so easy for me to go right back into my career because of Robert. He understands my work environment and he knows what it means to me. He would never have asked me or pressured me to give it up. He never made me feel guilty for not being at home. Without the support I received from him, I don't know how I would have made it handling a baby and a career. He never said "this is your role and this is mine." He respected my independence and my freedom to choose. Our attitude toward parenting Melissa is the result of the openness in our lives. We chose to share our lives together, and so we share every part of our lives as two rather than one. He has definitely made it easier for me, and as a result I am more self-assured—a positive feeling which I take back into my relationship with him. Neither of us is insecure about ourselves, our roles, or our relationship. I'm doing what I want to do and so is Robert. The housewife who feels frustrated because she isn't working or isn't fulfilled is experiencing much more tension and stress than I ever do as a working mother.

Support is a critical element in successfully balancing a career and family. Women are entitled to have what men have come to expect from others in their lives.

The stress of being a working mother is time-consuming and tiring. The feelings and issues which confront mothers who work are sometimes unfair and only serve to add to the burdens they already carry. However, if mothers feel they are supported in their efforts to pursue their field of interest, as men do, and combine this pursuit with a family, as men do, their opportunities for achieving a successful combination of the two lives are greatly enhanced. In order to feel that success, a mother must first feel some degree of inner peace about her life—the structure of her life as manifested through her progress toward goals she hopes to achieve in her career as well as in her personal life. It is helpful, though not essential, that a woman has the support of her family. If she is independent and determined she will probably succeed no matter what others may say. However, most women who work would admit that the support of a husband and family would be welcome.

Working mothers will admit that their children are more important than their work. Yet why should they be asked to choose when men are expected to place the needs of their jobs as top priority? The child of a working mother can feel the confidence and security from a mother who lets that child know that he or she comes first, that he or she is sincerely and deeply loved.

In storybook legends, a mother turned to her own mother for support. Grandmothers and older sisters were consulted for problems and support. The extended family is no longer a common source of support due to mobility. Support systems have had to be shifted to whomever is immediately available. Personal friends, professionals, or paid support in many cases are having to fill old functions and in so doing they are establishing new traditions.

AND WHAT ABOUT
THE CHILDREN?

Volumes have been written and thousands of words spoken about the issue of separating mother and child. Views of many of the contributing individuals reflect more about their values than actual unbiased data. Some experts feel that adults have romanticized the importance of mother being at home with freshly baked cookies or the aroma of bread baking when the children return from school. Some children like to visit other children after school, to run and romp and enjoy the freedom they could not experience during a structured day at school. Children want to pursue their own interests or special adventures—being alone, reading, climbing, hitting a ball against a wall, or taking a piano lesson. The issue is not whether a mother is home with cookies but whether or not the children are safe to pursue their needs and find outlets for their energies. If there is a responsible person around to see to the safety of the children, then the mother's presence is not so critical as some people would think. Part of the children's ability to pursue their interests lies in the security of knowing where their mother is and what she is doing. They usually will have little difficulty in filling their time until her return to the nest.

The most sensitive problem of working parents is deciding how to handle childcare. In many cases, the decision is made solely by the mother. Logistics have been given to the mother to work out as well as the often frustrating search for help.

Many working mothers feel that they must be the only one to handle childcare because, after all, the children have been their accepted responsibility. In addition, in order to justify working, the "problem" of the children must be managed. This is true for all women whether their children are very young or teenaged or whether they are in jobs that pay well or very little.

Though continuity is important in caring for children, other arrangements are sometimes needed to make ends meet. A location center in the home with each child's schedule for the week has been helpful to many working mothers in planning necessary arrangements and supervision.

Other mothers have found college students to be helpful. The benefit of students, if their schedules can be arranged, lies in the willingness of the students to "do things" with the children. The age difference is not as great as it is with an older housekeeper and the student is seen as a playmate "just for me." College students can play games with the children and take them to movies or special events. The patience of students will usually last long enough to entertain the children and is a change of pace for both the children and the student.

Many mothers have tried a cooperative approach to childcare, but again much planning must be done ahead of time. Several mothers will join together to form playgroups and have a "teacher" to supervise the children. This type of arrangement can be quite beneficial for working mothers. The children can be picked up at preschool, for example, and taken to a central neighborhood location. As a group, they lose feelings of fear and shyness and become "best friends" or a "club." These special playgroups can seem like a real treat to children if arrangements and supervision are satisfactory. Many schools have organized after-school programs that have been developed by parents.

Child-rearing is different for the working mother. There is no doubt about it. But it does not have to be one problem after another. Arrangements can be made by someone else to care for the children's needs, at least for some part of the day. Real concerns and problems, as well as joys and excitement, can usually wait until the mother or father or both get in the door.

For those who fear that their children will turn to the housekeeper or babysitter instead of the mother, research clearly indicates this is not the case. Jerome Kagan, a child development researcher from Harvard, found in a 1977 study that children turned for comfort to their biological mothers rather than to nurses or care-givers who spent more time with them. This strong tie was shown equally by children of working mothers and children reared by mothers at home.

Children do grow up like their parents. This does not ignore a temporary influence of a particular care-giver on certain behaviors. But children learn to act and talk like their mothers and fathers.

Where the child spends his time and with whom is less significant than the messages and feelings communicated by the mother. Many women go to endless lengths to make arrangements for their children, and even when they are home from work, their tireless tasks continue. Children pick up this pattern and know intuitively that the mother is taking care of their needs, but they are confused about why the father can relax with slippers and newspapers in his favorite chair while mother continues to "work."

Motherhood and fatherhood are just not the same. Fathers do help— with the children and with the house. Many studies have shown that fathers are more likely to share childcare than housework, and fathers with higher levels of education are more likely to spend time with their children. Women, however, are traditionally given responsibility for custodial tasks, whereas fatherhood represents interaction with the children. In the word-association game, more people give answers such as "cook," "clean," "care" to the term *mother* than to *father*. In association with the word *father*, answers fall into the "talk," "play," or "strong" categories. Fathers are not seen as the custodians of the children; thus they do not assume the "mothering" role unless prodded to do so. Both mothers and fathers fall into sex-stereotyped parenting roles.

Some fathers are willing to help if the requested activities do not interfere with their own plans. Jan works as a technologist at a hospital in the Northwest. She works from 7:00 A.M. to 3:00 P.M., and in order to take care of her mothering role, she gets up at 5:30, arranges three-year-old Janet's clothes, gets her breakfast on the table, and leaves for work by 6:30. Her husband does not like to be the one to administer "negative feelings" to the child; consequently he leaves all reprimanding to Jan. He wants the time spent with little Janet to be consistently positive. He dresses Janet, enjoys breakfast with her, and then drives her to nursery school. Jan picks her up about 3:15 and does the marketing and any other errands that need to be done. Then she goes home and starts dinner. During this time, she tries to talk to Janet about her day. As she does kitchen chores and the evening meal, she tries to "play" with Janet. Sometimes this is impossible because in order to get everything done that needs to be done, Jan must not stop her chores. Her husband gets home around 5:30 or 6:00 P.M. After dinner, the father plays with Janet while Jan again is working in the house. However, her husband feels he is "doing Jan a favor" by keeping Janet out of her hair while she works. What a favor! And neither of the parents stops to think why the father has the time to relax and play while the mother does not.

Women continue to feel guilty and overburdened. Caretaking mothers leave fathers free to have fun with or without the children.

A Break with Tradition

Traditionally, women have held all family responsibilities except one, that of breadwinner. Today, a majority of the millions of working women are also carrying that responsibility. Men have not had to think about their families because tradition assigned those tasks to women. Even if the children got sick, it seemed to fall on the woman to leave her job to stay with the sick children. Men could not risk having someone say, "What kind of man are you, staying home with a sick child? Let your wife do that. After all which comes first, your job or your family?" Men are told their job comes first. They must be part of the team and must do it before age forty. After all, the wife can take care of the children at home. Everyone needs a good wife. As the old saying goes, every successful man has a wife to tell him what to do and a secretary to do it.

Fortunately, there are a few men in the new generation who would be proud to stay home with sick children and risk being "laughed out of the office." Problems must be handled as needs arise, and men have their family problems just as women do. The difference is that most men do not say anything about their problems.

Many mothers prefer a well-trained day-care staff to family arrangements for preschoolers. However, only 19 percent of those who seek day care find openings. Instead children are left with neighbors or sitters costing anywhere from $1.50 an hour to $150 or more a week for a housekeeper. About two million of these children are "latchkey" children who come home to empty houses.

Parents who either cannot find or cannot afford day care must sometimes settle for temporary though painful adjustments. Many working mothers rely on their own mothers, in-laws, aunts, or other family members for support. Children are sometimes passed around when permanent arrangements cannot be made. In the South, one woman who wanted to complete her college degree was forced to leave her three children with their grandmother for two years. She could not afford living quarters for herself and her children so they were separated by two hundred miles while she lived in a dormitory. She had no alternative if she was to finish her formal training at that time. "I don't know how I made it through that period of my life," she confides, "but I was determined to make a better life for myself and my children and a college degree was the first step in that direction."

Even for those who are more affluent and can afford to hire a housekeeper, problems and frustrations arise. Without a back-up support system, a working mother is totally dependent on her babysitter. When the sitter fails to show, gets sick, or proves unreliable or inadequate, mothers face the dilemma of missing work, taking the children with her, or begging for help. Finding a dependable housekeeper is a recognized problem. Many women have devised their own systems or childcare, ranging from two or more college students during the week, students or couples who are willing to sit overnight or on weekends, or neighbors and church friends who volunteer to assist in emergencies.

Domestic duties have shifted from housecare to childcare, which requires a diversity of skills for the home childcare worker. Such workers have been in short supply, and many working mothers, in desperation, have mistakenly hired such workers without carefully checking references. Jessica, a researcher in the Midwest, ran through five homecare workers during the first quarter of last year. One, she found, was smoking marijuana around the children and another let the children roam unsupervised around the neighborhood while she talked on the telephone.

A change in attitude regarding the rigidity of maternal childcare is a necessity for the coming decade. Job sharing, flexible work schedules, and changes in the traditional male role are possible directions for improvement in the dilemma of getting childcare support for working mothers. Most men are not ready to forfeit the traditional male role and most companies are not willing to assist in accomodating those who try. Companies still reward the man who works diligently from seven in the morning to seven at night. However, many companies are now recognizing the national trend against relocating at the will of the company. Employees are more willing to look for another job than to keep moving.

Many companies have founded on-site day-care centers for employees. The results are often manifested in better morale, retention of experienced employees, and less absenteeism among the workers. Day-care costs can be amortized over a five-year period, which provides additional incentive to enter the day-care business. Some companies have tried variations of day-care centers, such as contracts with community centers or voucher plans for reimbursement.

Employers have traditionally expected female employees to be temporary. Until laws were passed making it illegal to ask female employees about their plans regarding babies and childcare, employers consistently used this information against women, placing them in dead-end positions, indeed, if they were hired at all.

Day-Care, Childcare, I Care

In America, a stratified childcare system exists with government-sponsored childcare for the poor, private childcare for the rich, and no childcare for middle America.

Working mothers do not dump their children at cold institutions and proceed with their own affairs. On the contrary, they go to great lengths to see that their children are well cared for while they work. Settings called day-care centers are simply not enough. Mothers want to know their children are in family settings with well-trained staff members. They want to be assured their children receive more than just adequate care and structured learning or play experiences.

Many homes do not have the facilities for the exploration toddlers need. So the three- to five-year-old is increasingly apt to attend some type of nursery school. This is true whether their mothers work or not. Pre-primary education has come to be regarded as valuable for all children regardless of culture or working status.

Almost every industrialized country except the United States has a national program for childcare. The French have a free kindergarten for children over three, state-licensed agencies that place children with volunteer sitters, and a large number of professional nannies. The Soviet Union serves thirteen million children in day-care centers by assignment. In Sweden, the government provides day care and pays 90 percent of the parent's salary (either parent) for a year to stay home with the baby.

The commitment in Sweden is based on the priority of full equality of sexes. Nonworking housewives are considered parasites and subjected to tax penalties. Of women with children, 60 percent have jobs—not that much higher than in the United States. Some companies even have night-care facilities in Sweden.

Most American women who work are in traditional fields for "women only," such as secretary or salesclerk. Their jobs do not yield the power that could demand and get childcare for workers. Only 17 percent of women laborers are in unions, which hardly would influence day-care programs for children.

Childcare is still essentially viewed as the female responsibility. Traditionally in American culture, children have been given to the charge of the wife and mother. The mother has been the one and usually the only one to cope with daily issues and problems concerning their care. Yet children do have two parents who are equally responsible for their well-being. Some fathers may think they know little or nothing about the care of young children. Our system has never given them a chance to learn by experience. The traditional family system is designed to shift the burden of childcare onto the mother. Because this role is assigned to the mother, men are prevented from sharing parenthood.

The research on the effect of childcare is inconclusive. Some findings seem to indicate that day care is neutral; other research points out that intelligence scores of infants in day care were higher than those at home. Psychologists generally agree that one-to-one contact is the crucial factor in the emotional development of children. However, relinquishing this nurturing role to someone else is difficult for many mothers and it results in strong feelings of guilt.

Cindy, a bank teller in the Northeast who needed her salary to support herself and her three-year-old son, found a nonprofit day-care center lodged in a church founded by community residents. The teachers were well trained and the ratio of adults to children was the recommended one to six. "It costs a little more than some programs and I have farther to drive," she said, "but it's worthwhile for Josh." Hours ranged from a half day to a full eight hours, depending on the parent's needs. Lessons for children aged two to six included storytelling, numbers, music, play, and nature study.

Another factor to be considered in planning for childcare is the number of hours a school or play center is open. Many centers keep banker's hours and thus no provision is made for parents who work until 5:00 P.M. Location of the school and transportation can also be eliminating factors for mothers who must depend on themselves for getting the child to and from school and for picking up children when they come down with a sniffle or a fever.

Childcare cannot be mass produced. As the number of children increases in a facility so does the need for teachers, administrators, and support personnel. Thus the cost per child increases and there is no positive correlation with the quality of care the child receives.

Perhaps the most plausible arrangement is the family care concept wherein a small number of children (up to six) of like nature are kept in a home by a warm mothering or fathering person. This arrangement makes sense economically as well. Usually the supervising adult enjoys being with the children and receives pleasure from administering care to them. The children in turn are provided with the stimulation of play with each other, different toys, an assortment of experiences, outdoor play in a safe area, proper food, and rest.

Once children enter school, their day is no longer dependent on the mother or the need for a mother figure. The main part of their day is spent in school. Childcare becomes the set of needed arrangements which must be made for before- or after-school hours. Many neighborhoods or communities have organized after-school programs. Some of these are held at the school with a teacher or college student supervising the children at the expense of the parents.

Children rarely change their after-school activities whether their mothers work or not. In a census survey in 1976, it was found that children of poorer families were more likely to be taken care of by a relative while their mothers worked, whereas families whose income was over $15,000 were more apt to have the children care for themselves.

Children of both sexes who have been exposed to a competent woman who combined the role of affectionate mother and intellectually active professional tend to be well-adjusted individuals. No woman should be placed in the position of choosing between her career and her children. Yet society unfairly forces that choice on thousands of women every day. A competent mother can manage a dual career and family life, and her children will usually be normal and well-adjusted with positive self-esteem.

The claim that children of working mothers become more self-reliant is an issue of frequent debate. There is no hard evidence to support either side unequivocably. Some mothers who feel this is true suggest that their children learn self-reliance, learn to accept responsibilities around the house and with siblings, and have a better relationship with their parents. However, it cannot be proven that children of working mothers, as a group, help more around the house than those whose mothers are there to supervise.

Career mothers feel that working provides self-satisfaction, which in turn makes them better mothers. This in fact is a claim more easily substantiated by research. Many counselors and pediatricians are more willing now than in the past to approve this line of thought. Mothers are now more able not only to realize but to freely admit that they dislike staying home or that their children literally drive them into a nervous frenzy. Many professionals feel that mothers who go to work for this reason may actually improve their relationship with their children.

Some mothers resent the implications inherent in dependence on the male for monetary support. There is a degree of respect which results from becoming financially independent or a contributing member of the family. Mothers who adhere to the position believe it is harmful for their children to see the mother in a position of servitude and lesser worth than the father. This indeed is a valid fear. There are many documented cases of children who, upon reaching adulthood, remember their mother as a slave.

Along the same line is the thought that a woman who works is a stronger role model for her daughter than one who does not enter the work force. Sons and daughters alike pattern their thinking about their own roles and the roles of future spouses on what they have seen as children. The vision of open opportunities for their own lives develops from experience and example. Children cannot be expected to be doers or to be active in society if their role models are passive.

Not surprisingly, the more positive effects that working seems to show benefit girls who see a female role model of high self-reliance and self-esteem. Daughters of working mothers have been found to have greater educational and career aspirations. They show higher academic achievement and more assertiveness and independence. They are also less rigid about sex roles.

The problem of childcare is compounded by proponents of the "family unit." The position taken by extremists is that the family is threatened by working mothers. This sentiment has been the force behind the defeat of government-sponsored or supported childcare facilities. Inherent in this philosophy is the assumption that there is no substitute for the real mother. Of course, this is a widely debated issue and will continue to be so.

The enjoyment and satisfaction of career opportunities are sometimes offset by the new set of conflicts at home. The day-to-day work load of a working mother can be altered by a preoccupation with efforts to balance childcare and work responsibilities. The shifting of child-rearing to the already complicated schedule of a working woman can detract from her focus on task and sap her working energy.

The success of a working mother depends on how satisfactorily she manages to arrange for the care of her children. Just as parenting is a series of routines and experiences, so childcare is a set of arrangements. It is rarely perfect, but maintaining satisfaction and consistency is a critical element in making childcare efforts successful.

The next decade holds many challenges for women in regard to change. Women themselves must be open to change in family roles, and they must be willing to shift some responsibility to the other parent. The issue of childcare is not just a woman's problem, it is a worker's problem. The institutions of home and work must be restructured to incorporate changing needs of society and include men as well as women.

FEELING GUILTY

The guilt and the go-it-alone grind are achingly familiar to millions of American women. They are trapped in the squeeze, the constant pressure to juggle home, family and job.

As more and more women enter the labor market for various reasons, emotional conflicts about work and feelings of guilt become common bonds for mothers in the work force. More women work than stay home. Working wives for the first time in history outnumber housewives. However, as a special group, working mothers are unrecognized and thus are not influential enough to make demands. There is power in numbers, but working mothers have not organized to wield a representative voice and voting power for millions of American women.

In 1980, almost six million mothers of preschool children worked. This group represents the fastest growing segment of the work force. They leave seven million children to be cared for while they earn money. Licensed day-care facilities absorb some of the seven million. Two-thirds are left with relatives, babysitters, nursery schools, or in some cases, alone. Because of this void in childcare facilities, women are forced to make agonizing decisions which result in emotional conflicts and extreme guilt.[2]

Whether they work by choice or necessity, mothers experience guilt in leaving their children in the care of others. Working mothers feel pangs of separation. The guilt focuses on all they have heard and felt as they grew up and listened to mothers, aunts, grandmothers, teachers, and other adult role models. The seeds for emotional conflict were planted early and blossom in full force when women are confronted with choices that men are not asked to make. The balance that women must achieve in order to feel inner peace is unrealistic and is much more difficult than any demands placed on men. Women are consistently asked to set their own feelings and ambitions aside in favor of the inherent and traditional duties of motherhood. Psychological stress is used against a working mother. A woman is made to feel negative about her personal desires if those desires conflict with tradition. She is left with ambivalent feelings about the development of her own talents—something never asked or expected of men. Men are culturally prepared to be ambitious and goal-oriented. They are taught to identify their talents and strengths and develop them to the fullest. Then men are expected to "settle down," marry, have children, and look to their wives to fulfill the needs of the family.

Women, by nature, have talents equal to those of men. The strengths possessed by women are as varied and individualized as any set of talents in a given group of men. Skills and talents are individual, not gender-related. Any society or set of people who assigns talents on the basis of sex is, as Plato said, using only half the resources of the state.

Working mothers have a strong fear that their children will suffer from maternal neglect and this fear is encouraged by society in general and other women in particular. Some men have contributed to these strong feelings of guilt. However, women have been better able to confront these allegations from men than from women. Perhaps women expect men to disagree with their career pursuits in combination with motherhood and they are better prepared to deal with the conflicts.

---

[2] Ann Oakley, *Woman's Work: The Housewife, Past and Present* (New York: Pantheon Books, a division of Random House, Inc., Copyright © 1976), pp. 210-211.

Other women, however, push their beliefs on working mothers without timidity, no matter how unfounded. Some of these beliefs include: (1) Women who have children ought to stay home and care for them. (2) Children should not be raised by babysitters, housekeepers, or maids. The values, language, and habits of the children will reflect their keepers, not their parents. (3) It is selfish of a mother to spend time away from her children. After all, children are only young once and they grow up so fast. (4) The mother-child bond of early childhood is the most important relationship a child will ever have. If children have a strong bond with their mothers, their problems will be few.

Fears are instilled into the working mothers and these fears continue to be perpetuated by nonsupportive groups. Negative statements are passed around about mother substitutes, and negative research is exaggerated about the consequences of working motherhood on the child. Mother substitutes help children learn to extend their feelings beyond their mothers and to care for other adults. The results of this can be greater independence for the child, increased capacity to love, and a faster maturity rate.

Women are a vital part of contemporary change in society. The nineteenth century defined women as the keepers of moral virtues. They were duly appointed moral superiors to men in the home. These domestic women of the world founded ideals and reforms on which social purity was based, including mass movements against prostitution and temperance. Thousands of these mother superiors worked without guilt every day. Yet they were not criticized because their jobs related to the family.

Some twentieth-century women fall into the same category. Although dubbed *homemakers*, they work daily and diligently to stamp out equal rights, homosexuality, abortion, nuclear energy, and war. They have made full-time professions out of defending homemaking. And where are the children of these "homemakers"? Many of them are kept in the same places as children of working mothers.

Some women use issues to get involved outside the home because they really do not want to be in the home. This has served to justify working outside the home by defending its very foundation. In traditional homes and traditional marriages, the woman who crusades for her family is less likely to be criticized than the woman who crusades for her own rights.

Many women believe it is their personal responsibility to raise the children; thus they have ambivalent and guilty feelings about another person caring for their children. They feel unsure about whether or not their children are being hurt by their desire to work. They have been conditioned since their own childhoods that a mother's place is in the home. This myth, tempered by the attitudes and confusion of contemporary women, perpetuates itself.

Some women have solved this series of conflicts by choosing to remain childfree. In such circumstances women are saying, in essence, that they refuse to go along with the single parent responsibility of raising children.

Caroline, who had been working for several years, said she did not have regrets about leaving her two children with other adults at an early age.

I think it's one of the best things I ever did for my children. They became accustomed to other adults and learned to tolerate flexibility rather than to have everything as they would always like it. Let's face it. Life is like that. I would not be a good mother if I let my children believe everyone would oblige their demands. So, I'm teaching them to adjust to many people and their personalities seem to be much more easy going than some children whose mothers do everything for them.

Sure, it hurt me when the baby would cry when I left in the morning occasionally. But I knew they were telling me they cared about me, not the sitter. They know who mother is. There is no doubt about that. I never had the slightest jealousy that my children preferred a sitter or got too attached. I was happy they had learned to love more people and their extended family was greater than other children because of those feelings. The suggestion that a hired person could replace family feelings is ridiculous. Parents who fear strong ties outside the family must be insecure. I think experiences with other adults are enriching for children. The short amount of time spent with others compared to the years, weekends, and nights spent with parents is not threatening in the least.

Much of the guilt women experience is the result of conditioning. Understanding the difference between natural feelings and conditioned feelings is very difficult, especially since women have been made to feel negative and selfish when their own feelings are recognized.

Maternal behavior varies among women. Some are capable of being good mothers but simply cannot maintain a vigil over the crib. Not all mothers magically sense the solutions to the needs of their children. All women do not enjoy spending time with babies or reading to toddlers. Some mothers relate better with children who are older. Children whose mothers do not enjoy caretaking and nurturing are actually better off in the attentive, loving care of a sitter, nurse, or housekeeper. Children who are hyperactive and nervous need a structured schedule. The needs of children such as these are more adequately met in a structured day-care program. The fact is, not all mothers or children should stay at home. The old cultural fantasy about living in suburbia with the station wagon, two children, and a dog and caring for home and husband happily ever after is just that—a fantasy. Just like the clean, sweet-tempered baby who never spits up or cries, the fairy tale is rare in real life.

Overcompensation
and Insecurity

The working mother must always be careful of her time allotment with the children. It is true that children need attention from loving parents, but that may not always be possible. When one parent is absent from the home for whatever reason, the remaining parent must be sensitive to the child's needs.

Some working mothers tend to overcompensate for their absences. This can cause the child to be overly dependent on a mother. Although overcompensation may be the by-product of maternal guilt, it perpetuates the myth that being away from your child is being a bad mother. The behavior rooted in guilt results in a feeling which seems almost patronizing to children. A mother might continuously ask, "What do you want to do?" Children catch on to this behavior pattern and learn to use it as a tool to get the upper hand on parents, particularly a working mother.

Mothers who work may feel at times apologetic about going to work. They worry that their children will experience insecurity. A working mother may behave passively as she compromises, lingers, soothes, and re-assures her children. Instead of this behavior, her energies could be more effectively directed toward positive output if she would spend the time allotted to her children in loving moments. Such experiences serve to draw her children closer to her as she builds strong positive two-way communication. Many mothers assume that their children are opposed to the idea of a mother who works outside the home. In so doing, mothers keep their children from learning to accept that fulfillment is a need of both their parents. Mothers continue to perpetuate the "woman's place" when they undercut male attempts to be a parent. This happens when they insist that the mother is the only person capable of attending the children's needs.

At home mothers do not always plan uninterrupted time periods devoted to their children. They seem to feel that just being in the house is spending time with the children. Because of this, many children whose mothers do not work actually receive less attention from their mothers than the children of mothers who do work and structure their schedules.

Studies show that working mothers spend almost as much time with their children as mothers who are at home. Specific studies of working mothers such as those conducted by Lois Hoffman found that working mothers read more often to their children and were more likely to plan activities based on their children's interests.

Working mothers tend to spend more time with their children during their off hours, evenings, and weekends than nonworking mothers. They rarely use babysitters and spend weekend time conscientiously with the children. Much of this is compensation time but the children do benefit from the attention. They are not neglected as myth would indicate. They learn to accept the parents' schedules and to adapt, an important skill for living in comtemporary society.

Nonworking mothers are apt to put their children to bed early so that less time is shared if the father is present. Childcare is arranged at odd hours, usually to give the nonworking mother time for her own pursuits. Babysitters and weekends away from the children amount to, in many cases, as much or more time away as the working mother. This is not the same kind of flexibility that a child needs in order to learn adaptation to life. The difference is in the lack of consistency involved. The working mother usually provides a schedule of work and childcare with a degree of consistency, and a child learns to adjust. However, many nonworking mothers do not realize that schedules and impulse absences may be harmful to young children. The child never knows when the mother is leaving or returning. The child does not learn to trust the exit and entrance because the variation is confusing and often too frequent or too long. Child psychologists have said for years that children learn security from consistent behavior. Thus the consistency of a structured schedule or planned time together seems to provide for the needs of children better than the flexible schedule of a nonworking mother.

There has always been a continuing debate between quality of time and quantity of time and most experts agree that the quality of time spent with children is more important. It is important for children to feel that their mother is really responding to them, really giving attention to them rather than dividing it among numerous chores or activities for which a mother is responsible.

Women who work outside the home are not worse mothers than full-time mothers because they work. There is no magical assurance that children will receive a special gift by the mother's presence in the home.

Employed mothers are only, after all, doing what women have done throughout history and in all cultures, which is to participate in the economically productive life of society. The essential variables so far as children are concerned are the quality of the care they receive and the mother's attitudes to her job, not the fact of employment on its own. . . . But the myth of motherhood takes its toll. Employed mothers often feel guilty. They feel inadequate, and they worry about whether they are doing the best for their children. They have internalized the myth that there is something their children need that only they can give them.

Both the working and nonworking mother must learn to let their children trust them by developing in them a strong sense of love and security. Love is not based on carpools, lunch box treats, rainy day afternoons, and the answer to "what can I do now?" Love between a parent and child is an assurance that no matter where one or the other is, the trust and feeling of importance persists. A mother who works, as well as one who does not, needs to believe this and have confidence in herself so that she can teach this trust to her children.

Learning to build a trusting relationship is not easy because of the psychological stress of continual career conflicts and the perpetual myths surrounding motherhood in society. The contemporary woman who is not accustomed to thinking about trust relationships with children may underestimate the importance of developing such relationships, and she may easily misjudge the positive influence such strength can add to her career. Women experience conflict over their role because of the issue of whether or not they ought to work. They are made to feel guilty about their jobs. Yet societal attitudes are different for working mothers who are poor. The alternative of becoming a welfare recipient justifies the "sacrifice" of the

[3]Jean Curtis, *A Guide for Working Mothers* (New York: Doubleday, 1976), p.31.

children—so poor working women are encouraged to feel they are doing the right thing. They are not made to feel guilty.

Maxine, a working mother with two boys, reported that it took a long time for her to realize that psychological guilt was an unnecessary part of mothering.

I have to travel some in my job and each time I had a trip I would organize every detail at home for the boys and my husband before I left. Things were very smooth when I was away because all the family had to do was follow the list I had prepared. I realized it was too simple. Why couldn't they do this on their own without all the time I had to spend preplanning? I felt a drive within to get all the routines organized. I realized that it was to compensate for my own guilt of being away, and I had to convince myself that my mothering continued even in my absence. The men I worked with didn't carry lingering domestic feelings on business trips and I knew my husband never worried about the house, the children, or me while he was gone. So why was I unable to make the break between domestic and professional lives? Once I was able to come to grips with my guilt, I was able to cope with it. I talked to some friends and decided to try to rid myself of this psychological guilt. I began by talking to the boys about my being away. To my astonishment, they were not bothered. They knew when I was coming home and why I had to leave. They knew me as their mother and they trusted what I said. Furthermore, I had been actually depriving them of planning for themselves. Shame on me! I had stolen from their father the opportunity to learn how to provide for their needs, too. I was the one who had been feeling bad about leaving, not them. I was the one who felt like staying near them, but it was my need—not theirs! What a revelation. My husband could go off on the subway or plane and forget. I could not and it was only hurting me and my work. The family never suffered. Now I let them plan everything: housecleaning, schedules, marketing, and they've learned so much. I'm embarrassed at my failure to let go because I had considered myself a "liberated" female.

Kitchen Guilt

Another woman, who worked as a personnel manager in a large corporation said that her guilt fell in the category of kitchen guilt.

I had a terrible nagging guilt that my family would develop scurvy or some dreadful disease if I didn't prepare inviting and nutritious meals every night. I just couldn't wean myself away from those feelings about my duties in the kitchen. Call it guilt if you like but it was really strong. I equated meal preparation with the proper execution of my motherhood responsibilities. My husband and children would see a whole new world open up if something should happen to me. They would see that vegetables don't just magically appear on the table and that meals aren't events that occur without planning. I have always baked a lot for the family, especially breads. I guess my grandmother got me started on that when I was young. I remember her kneading the dough and I remember the wonderful aroma from the oven. She used to tell me it was a part of loving your family. So I grew up thinking that no matter what else I did for myself, I owed that to my family. I've continued to keep the responsibilities all to myself, not because I wanted to do everything, but because I felt the responsibilities were mine, not my children's or my husband's. I've even been known to feel guilt pangs at serving frozen prepared foods—I've changed the container the food was heated in and put it in my dishes so my family wouldn't know I hadn't cooked it myself!

My husband wouldn't have the slightest idea how to carry on without me. He would be amazed at the ants which frequent the floor of the kitchen, the order in which the dishes must be placed in the dishwasher, and the budget-stretching which has been done in marketing for the week. He wouldn't know that clothes must be sorted before being washed, or that special words must be uttered to Barry when he gets a scrape on his knee. He wouldn't know that Rachael's back must be rubbed in a special way when she wakes up at 3:00 A.M. He doesn't hear their sounds or footsteps during the night like I do. He wouldn't know how to get a direct answer out of the pediatrician or how to balance green and yellow vegetables. But he needs to know because if I should die tomorrow he couldn't possibly learn everything in time to keep the family going.

Psychological stress can be transformed into feelings of guilt. Certain aspects of mothering, such as kitchen guilt, can be the result of emotional stress. Many working mothers admit that they continue to feel more responsibility for the children than their husbands, even though the father of the children could contribute to their well-being. Mothers are reluctant to let go of that intuitive feeling to make sure their seats are securely buckled and make sure that each child receives the proper daily supply of vitamins and proteins. The role is difficult to relinquish. Women have continued to perpetuate the helplessness of men by lowering their expectation for total responsiblity in shared parenting. After conception, many women see the mother-child relationship exclusive of the male. Many fathers are not asked to participate in the stages of pregnancy and may never meet the obstetrician until the birth is announced in the waiting room. They are left out of the unforgettable experiences prior to and during the birth of their children. This is the beginning of their exclusion from the child-rearing years. Many fathers hesitate to step into parenting opportunities without a specific invitation. Women are convinced their husbands cannot care for the children in the same way and they transfer the lack of confidence to men. Such expressions as, "Here, let me do that" or "I might as well take care of it myself" or "*I've* always done that" tend to put men on the defensive in regard to offering parental services or sharing responsibilities.

Programmed to Feel Guilty

Women presume that they alone know how to care for their children. This conditioned assumption begins before birth when women keep "secrets" and feelings to themselves or dismiss them from possible communication because they think their husbands "just wouldn't understand" what they're going through. Women may gain a baby in the process of birth but they lose a sense of freedom from that moment forward. The feeling of responsibility, if taken alone, which many mothers expect, is an awesome one for the days ahead as head of childcare. The feeling is absorbed into the mother's total being so that, without question, she accepts the responsibilities ahead as hers.

Few events have greater impact on a woman's life than becoming a mother. The image she has of herself changes. The vulnerability of her decisions increases as her emotions lie cuddled in her arms. The long career climb to success suddenly looks longer as a mother feels burdened, yet not unexpectedly or negatively, by the lifelong set of responsibilities she has silently accepted and symbolically presented to her mate.

There has been a decline in the economic value of the traditional role of women. The significance of the past has been lessened. Caring for the young is for a limited time. Managing a household has declined as a socially useful skill. One buys those things that a generation ago were made at home. Food is processed and frozen so cooking has become less time consuming.

Women have laughed among themselves, their mothers, grandmothers, and aunts for years about the ineptness of men where raising children is concerned. They have almost managed to create a myth that masculinity and childcare do not go together. When men are left with children to raise, the myth prevails to such an extent that they are perceived as helpless and unfortunate. It is true that men may not know all the details involved in the complete role of parenting, but they are certainly capable of learning.

Many mothers feel that during work they should not talk about their children. This is based on the fear that they will be labeled "mothers" rather than professionals. They are anxious to prove they belong in the work force and that, no matter what, they can succeed.

Jo lived in a small town in southwest Ohio. She had worked in public relations during the early years of her marriage to Walter. Her job never seemed to either of them as important in prestige or salary as his. However, they both looked at her job as just that—a job, not a permanent career; Jo was not concerned with advancement because she knew that sooner or later she would be leaving. After five years of working, she quit to have a son and then a daughter. She was a conservative, low-keyed woman who expected the traditional role and never questioned her "duty" to stay home with the children. Jo and Walter lived in a small home, and after six years of staying home, she started to think about the extra money that her job could bring in. As soon as she mentioned her plans to Walter, he became furious.

"The children need you here. What about Walt when he gets home from school and what about Alice during the day? No wife of mine will work. Everybody would think I couldn't support my family. Besides I thought it was understood when we got married that you would give up your job when we had children."

Next, Jo got a call from her mother and finally from her mother-in-law, who insisted a visit to Ohio was in order to "talk things over." From both, Jo heard the same tale until she was deep in a sea of guilt for her thoughts.

"Your children need you," she was told. "You know a woman belongs in the home." Jo felt so bombarded that she dropped the idea. In less than a year, Walter had been laid off from his job and Jo offered to go to work. This time, Walter agreed. Six months later, he returned to work but Jo was enjoying her job so much she had no intention of quitting. She remembered what she had chosen to forget for the last seven years about working. Walter agreed that Jo could continue to work "providing everything stays the same at home."

Women who depend on approval from a man or from family members in order to make the choice to go to work or stay home can experience a great deal of conflict. Limitations are placed on them by husbands, parents, in-laws, or others who seem to be in a position to monitor, judge, or advise. Those who allow themselves to remain in a manipulated situation suffer silently while others around them are never fully aware of the dilemmas they face or the motivation behind their passivity. Women who find themselves in similar situations are allowing themselves to be manipulated and will never have control of their own lives. Why some women are willing to accept conditions regarding their career and motherhood is puzzling to say the least. Yet they obviously feel capable and willing to accept the double burden of work and housework on the premise of maternal guilt. They feel it is their responsibility and they are unwilling or unable to pull themselves out from under the traditional image. They allow themselves to be compromised and in so doing submit their careers to unequal value compared to a man. Child-rearing can serve as a security blanket, never drawing the inequality of a woman's career into open confrontation. Her career remains neatly and unquestioningly in the background and she pretends that it is nothing to work full time and maintain a family.

Many women have difficulty making a clear division of their thoughts between home and office. Thoughts about children or childcare arrangements are not constantly floating around in their minds. Women placed according to their abilities usually perform well on the job because women are certainly smart and ambitious. However, there is a strong overriding assumption that women belong at home and they must constantly defend why they are away from the nest.

Ambitious working mothers work very hard to be superior in the office and at home. They do not want to fail in either setting. They will not allow anyone to say that they are less than perfect mothers. They try to portray an image of perfection: the paragon of motherhood and the quintessence of professionalism.

When children of working mothers have problems, the assumption is made too often that it is the mother's fault. The children's problems are rarely attributed to the father's work or career choice. The mother's career receives the blame for everything, from the child's forgotten lunch box to adolescent traumas. Working mothers, however, do not feel that combining a career and a family is harmful.

Children of working mothers fail history tests and so do children of mothers who stay home all day. The six-year-old whose mother works and who is apprehensive about school for two months may not be any different from the six-year-old whose mother is at home baking chocolate chip cookies in preparation for his arrival at three o'clock. In *The Two Paycheck Marriage,* Caroline Bird states:

> *. . . a mother's job does not radically change the daily experience of children at any age. Studies have failed to establish any reliable correlation between the employment of a mother and the development of her children, and the testimony of children themselves is for the most part neutral.*

> *It turns out that children are less affected by whether their mothers work than they are by how their mothers feel about what they are doing. According to Lois Wladis Hoffman, satisfied women make good mothers. This means that a mother who likes her job is not going to do her child any favor by quitting to stay at home. Because she is home all day, she runs the risk of taking her dissatisfaction out on her child. Hoffman found that the children of reluctant homemakers who would rather work are worse off than the children of reluctant working wives who would rather be at home.*[4]

Ambivalent feelings are perfectly natural. It does not mean children are loved any less. It does mean a woman can now be honest and realistic about the demands on her personal life.

Some mothers feel guilty about the few pursuits they give themselves. Penny, married to an attorney, had a child early in her marriage and continued to teach school. She did not feel guilty about working, something she thoroughly enjoyed, but her feelings changed when she went back to school. "Somehow," she said, "I feel it's all right for me to be doing something when I'm getting paid for it. But the idea of spending time away from my child to have fun or go to school makes me feel terribly

---

[4]Caroline Bird, *The Two-Paycheck Marriage* (New York: Rawson Wade Publishers, 1979), p. 149.

guilty. I feel I am neglecting my son for myself." Her guilt stemmed from pursuits which she saw as beneficial to herself.

The burden of maternal guilt lies in the daily and hourly questioning of self. Am I doing what is right? Am I doing enough? Am I a good mother to my child? Am I doing too much?

The issue of a mother working is not nearly as important as the guilt a mother carries about working. It is the guilt, primarily, which can be the potential cause of damage to the child, the mother, the relationship. Aside from the obvious neglect of children, which few working mothers are guilty of, the worse effect felt by children of working mothers who feel guilty is overcompensation for their absence. Children who are victims of this are overindulged, are less socially mature, show less initiative and less cooperation, and demonstrate worse academic performance than children of mothers at home.

Well-adjusted children have mothers who are satisfied with themselves and with what they are doing. Studies of young children and adolescents have indicated similar results. The attitude of the mother—whether she is pleased with what she is doing or resentful, gratified or guilty—seems most important. The self-esteem, energy level, and feelings of personal worth can be derived from an executive job, a "pink collar" job, or homemaking. A woman's self-image and energy supply determines not only the quality of maternal behavior but also the message transmitted to her children about female competence and dignity.

SOCIAL RESTRICTIONS

Many women who are aware of their professional ambitions tend to modify these aspirations in the social world. They are careful not to seem too assertive or ambitious on the social scene. The pursuit of a feminine image seems to determine a woman's social inclinations. She tries to separate her womanly role from her professional role. The effect is one of a dual life—a work life and a home life.

The professional identity of a woman is often deliberately kept hidden, as if it were a secret. Communication of a woman's working status is rarely a part of social conversation, much less a focal point. In fact, a woman may feel herself limited professionally by her husband. His profession often sets the boundaries and expectations of her total role. In some relationships a woman may feel that her career by comparison is unimportant. In the social world of the couple, the female may feel her prestige accompanies her partner's career and that on her own merits she would not enjoy similar prestige.

Women have tended to settle for elements of the fairy tale envisioned in early childhood—a nice guy, enough money to maintain a certain standard of living, a reasonably happy home, and possibly some semblance of a career—if the home is not upset in the process. Newer generations of women have indicated they are not as easily satisfied. In search of a fuller life, a perhaps richer and more satisfying experience, contemporary women are more likely than their foremothers to set higher personal goals, to quest after dreams once never thought possible for women.

Socially, many women have been made to feel somewhat apologetic for not staying at home with the children. There have been aspersions cast on women who are labeled "ambitious" by lesser educated or envious friends. This negativism focuses on a theory of selfish ambition, which assumes that a career-minded woman really should not have children because she simply does not have time for them. For some women, this indeed is the case, but for those talented and assertive women who do marry and choose to have babies, the theory does not apply. Ambitious, talented men are not asked to forsake parenthood. Indeed, they are encouraged to become fathers. Women should not be asked to compromise their careers or to feel guilty for pursuing such a direction.

For many talented women, there is no choice in combining career and family. Determination is motivated by economic survival. These women certainly deserve to be supported in their efforts. Changes in attitudes are necessary to keep pace with history and society as times change.

Women of the current generation have reaped the benefits of consciousness-raising and antidiscrimination laws. Women who were making major life decisions before the benefits of the women's movement experienced the same conflicts. However, there was very little hope during earlier years that women could actually make choices regarding career and family. The real conflicts for those women were somewhat lessened because the restrictions were not only greater, they were unquestioned. Women felt obligated to stay home and raise their children while the husbands went to work. That role was universally expected of them and was supported by teachers who used textbooks showing Dick and Jane at home with Mom in the kitchen. The highlight of these exciting stories was the arrival of Dad home from work. Occasionally, the entire family might go out to buy shoes for Dick and Jane. Mother usually did not tackle such monumental decisions alone.

Throughout the life of Dick and Jane and others growing up in that era, the theme was concurrent. Mom stayed home and had babies. Dad pursued his career. Those women who married shelved ambitions and career desires or postponed their feelings until a more socially acceptable time. They never led independent lives. They went from the dependence of home and parents to the dependence of husbands without question.

Emily who grew up with mixed emotions during this period, experienced the traditional acculturation of society and as a result was more than hesitant to pursue her desire to study law.

I knew what my expected role was—from my parents, my teachers, other adult figures, and even my friends. I married very early, possibly hoping for a little more freedom. My hopes for freedom came to a grinding halt when I got pregnant. After the baby came, it was obviously my responsibility. My husband continued school, and his relationships with his single friends never seemed to change. Yet, for me, life was limited. I stayed home with the baby while he played golf. I began to feel resentful of my responsibilities and his freedom. I started back to school, part time at first, working toward my degree, but it seemed easy to put off my career with two children. My friends kept telling me I could always pick up a career later. I felt the old traditions pulling at me and my friends really made me feel worse during a decisive period. They kept telling me I should enjoy being a wife and a mother and stop thinking so much of my career.

Emily's friends tried to convince her that if she did not stay home with her children, the children would not be hers. The implication seemed clear that the children of her friends would experience closer family relationships, closer maternal ties, and might even be better adjusted than Emily's though this belief was without foundation. In other words, they simply were stating their adherence to the old either/or choice of working and children, which no doubt was supported by their own husbands. Why do "friends" insist on giving advice albeit well meaning? Quite likely, the issue is based on status. They were somewhat afraid that Emily would acquire greater status and leave them behind—that once Emily got into that big world of business, she would no longer have need of that particular group of friends. Even more than that, her success in business would shift attention to a comparison between her achievement and that of her friends.

Many women bear the same emotional burdens as Emily. The innuendos are planted by others. "The children won't have your values if they are raised by someone else." or "So and so works and look what problems she has with her children." There is no research which conclusively proves that children are more stable coming from homes where mothers work or remain at home.

Playing the Role

Some women who work have learned to limit the impact of their friends' advice. Many simply do not tell "friends" or social acquaintances what they are doing. One woman said the women who were her best friends would not really understand or appreciate her position in research at a nearby college, and so, she said, "I just don't mention my work when I'm around them."

Another woman says that when she is entertaining with her husband, she feels her primary role is that of wife. She is careful to avoid any references to her own achievement. "Not that what I do is more important, but I feel that among his friends, the glory should be his and I don't want him to feel I am competing for respect."

Shelly, a writer, never mentions her achievements socially. Most of her friends, she says, know little or nothing about her professionally.

As far as they are concerned, I am a mother or Edward's wife. Almost none know what I have achieved. I don't mention it because I don't want them to feel I am different."

I remember one night when Edward and I were having dinner with some friends—an accountant and his wife and a very well-to-do executive and his socially inclined wife. The night began as we were all sitting around having wine, and I noticed how much the men were dominating the conversation, as if only their comments were important. It was interesting, I thought, yet so typical that these wives were engrossed in "woman talk" and were quite satisfied to be excluded from the "men talk." I was sitting between two of the men during the conversation and one got up, saying, "We don't want to bore you. Why don't we change places so you can talk to the women?" I was completely surprised. Considering that my role that evening was wife and these were friends of my husband, I moved. Upon settling in his new seat, he then exclaimed, "Now we can talk seriously!" I said little until dinner when my husband brought up something about my work for women. This time, he turned and said to me, "Oh, you're one of those, eh? A libber!" He made the standard ridiculous comments such as "Well, men can't have babies, now, can they? Otherwise I'd be glad to stay home and have babies!" I'll just bet he would! Although there were two other women at the table, they said nothing in rebuttal of his putdown of women. In retrospect, perhaps they were smarter than I—knowing a verbal battle with the narrowminded is a waste of time. After that evening, I decided I would no longer be subjected to social situations which I considered demeaning and compromising to my values and beliefs, wifely role or not. I would never ask that kind of sacrifice of my husband and he shouldn't ask it of me. If he wants to see people like that socially, from now on he can go alone.

Many women who are involved in full professional pursuits are still feeling conflicts socially, and a large percentage of the time that conflict arises from communication with former friends who knew them before they became "professional." Facing the fact that career changes intrude into all areas of a woman's life is sometimes difficult. It is especially hard to recognize those changes which occur socially. However, as a woman's life changes, her social context does not remain unaffected. Friends may be envious, jealous, embarrassed, or afraid—feelings which are rarely expressed but common in existence. Lifestyles and interests have changed and, as a result, a woman may have less to talk about with old friends. The strain and tension are present, though unrecognized. Realizing and accepting the fact that friends, at least temporarily, may shift is difficult for the career woman.

Conflict by Implication

The controversy of mothers working is an issue which evokes strong feelings. People ask, "How do you manage to work with children and all there is to do?" No matter what answer is given the comment which follows is usually negative like, "That must be terribly difficult" or "Oh, I had a neighbor who had all kinds of problems trying to work and be a mother." By implication, they suggest the topic is one of strong opinion and that a person is either for or against working mothers in much the same way you are for or against abortion. And whichever side a woman takes, she is called on to defend herself, as Shelley did. Conflict evolves from this defensive act and feeling of skepticism.

Women who have worked for many years learn to harden themselves to social disapproval. A woman from Atlanta was asked if she worked, and on replying in the affirmative, was then confronted with "Oh, you do? What do you do with your children?" The obvious implication was "poor children." This woman was assertive enough to say "I neglect them, of course!"

Entertaining is another social restriction for a working mother. Not only does she face greater limitations on her time for planning and preparation, but she must combine entertaining with the complexity of guilt in dividing her time among her children, husband, and herself. Many times, she may want to have a dinner party, but she may feel a nagging guilt to spend that evening with the children. A working mother must be able sharply and accurately to assess the needs of the children and husband as well as being aware of her own. These needs can then be translated into priorities for dividing limited time so that she gets some time to spend as chosen. This is a process that can occur without guilt after some degree of practice in assessing needs and utilizing quality time management.

When that occasional dinner party does reach the table, guests who are aware of the working status of the hostess are somewhat bewildered that this "career woman" has domestic skills. What they really mean is, "Surely you must fail at something. It must be mothering and housekeeping." Again a working mother is so placed on the defensive that she might be motivated to go out of her way to prove she can cook and keep house. This "prove it" chip-on-the-shoulder attitude accomplishes little. The socializing becomes more difficult.

There is a feeling, a schism, between mothers who work and mothers who do not. Most mothers at home overtly feel that their children are better off than those of working mothers. This feeling is a natural one for it serves to justify not working. On the other side, mothers who do work know that the quality of the time spent with their children is more important than just being at home while the children sit in front of the television. Women who have returned to work from the ranks of homemakers often report a "feeling" of being different, somewhat of an invisible barrier. Most women notice this change of attitude quickly.

Accompanying this change is a feeling of loss of contact with old friends, mothers who stay home. A busier schedule of course, has much to do with this. There simply may not be free afternoons or leisurely lunch times to spend with a friend. Logistically, the working mother may be on a tight schedule to accommodate her job needs as well as the needs of her children. Opportunities to be with nonworking mothers are few.

A busy working mother soon finds that she may have to set aside time for seeing friends who are important to her. One couple hires a babysitter for Tuesday night. She visits friends and he goes bowling.

Some working women use commuting time to keep in touch by writing notes to friends with whom they otherwise would not have time to communicate. Other women follow the cue of their male counterparts and have lunch with friends and send flowers, gifts, or baked goods, sometimes at company expense. Expectations have changed for working mothers today. The ability to pursue social relationships is changing with the schedule and demands working mothers have to satisfy.

Eleanor admitted she seldom had time for her friends after she began a new job.

> *My children had to come first. I just didn't have time anymore to call friends on the telephone. They resented it I guess because they stopped calling me. Most of the relationships I used to have are gone and I'm sorry about it. The people I remained friendly with don't mind my working, but some people I had been friends with just don't understand the way I live and what I do. I feel somewhat isolated from social contacts I used to have but I think it's natural. Even some of my husband's friends are uncomfortable around me. I have as much education as they do, more in some cases, but they still won't treat me as an equal, worthy of intelligent conversation. My social contacts have changed and really so they should because I have changed too.*

Some changes in social relationships are more subtle. One set of restrictive attitudes comes from older women. Many of these women have stayed home during their childbearing years and resent the freedom mothers now have. They are guided by the old school of thought that "what was good enough for me, is good enough for them." Other women who have never had children are often unaware of the trials and tribulations of working mothers. These women are as chauvinistic as their male counterparts. They schedule meetings at their convenience or expect working mothers to exhibit the same flexibility in scheduling as a person with total freedom. A working mother rarely has freedom, but the restrictions she has are ones of choice. She chooses to be a mother and if she chooses to work it is because of the satisfaction of each and because she has the talents to combine both.

Women with children often view childfree women as having attitudes similar to those of stereotypic men. Some working mothers find childfree women to be unsympathetic, since they have no frame of reference for children or for scheduling responsibilities and needs. Furthermore, many working mothers encounter disapproval or resentment from some child-free women who are unconvinced that a working mother can manage it all—be superwoman, supermom, and supercareerwoman. However, such childfree women are usually unaware of the inherent sacrifices of free time, leisure, athletic or social activities, and perhaps of the lack of a sense of tranquility or inner peace.

Working mothers have also expressed the opinion that some childfree women appear to be threatened by mothers who seem to have it all—children, husband, home, family, ambition. Such mothers have chosen their way, plotted their future, stepped out of line. Working mothers may seem to others to have the privileges of a man's world.

Cecile started to notice a subtle change during the first six months after going back to work as an account executive in an advertising firm. She noticed that her house was messy, which was somewhat disturbing to her, but she was never good at house cleaning anyway. Then she began to feel uncomfortable socially because she was no longer included in some of the things she had participated in prior to her return to work—such as neighborhood get-togethers for the children at Halloween, end of the summer picnics, and Christmas caroling.

I sought out the women who had been casual acquaintances, though it was a effort on my part, and I was surprised to see our relationship had changed. I could no longer pick up where we had left off on our activities. I sensed the women weren't as relaxed with me. I discovered that plans had been made as usual and I was left out. Then I realized there was an unspoken criterion for membership in the group—the common bond of housewifery.

I really felt hurt yet I understand their actions. You make a choice in life and then you find others who have made the same choice (or similar) and you seek out each other. You feel more comfortable around those with common bonds.

Some women have always considered themselves as somewhat of an oddity in comparison with the norm. Leslie taught sociology at a college in the South. She had felt "different" because her range of activities was quite uncommon compared with the range of feminine activities of other mothers. Occasionally, she was asked to send cookies for a school party but never was asked to participate in a carnival, spaghetti supper, or help out in any school event.

> *I wondered if I was on a list somewhere with "Working Mother, Don't Ask" by my name. My son noticed this, too, and said, "Mom, why don't you ever come to my parties like Timmy's mom?" I didn't want to say "because I wasn't invited" so I made up an excuse. It is actually unfair how working mothers are categorized as nonparticipants. It seems to me someone is assuming that working mothers don't want to be included and that just isn't true.*

The assumption about working mothers is a fallacious one, yet many mothers believe it to be true. Some believe that working mothers are too busy and do not want to be bothered. Some feel that this is fact, not fiction. There may be a certain degree of resentment among housewives when they see working mothers being allowed to have the best of both worlds. Resentment may turn into anger if housewives see participation opportunities offered to working mothers first. Real conflict develops if schedules are arranged around those of working mothers. Why should working mothers be given first choice on conferences with teachers when housewives have busy schedules too? These hidden thoughts and feelings may never be overtly expressed. Yet the attitude and behavior of housewives toward working mothers clearly demonstrates that social relationships are affected. This behavior can be manifested in many ways. Exclusion from social events among couples is one way women "get even" with a working mother who might have more to talk about than mothers whose exposure is limited. Exclusion from planning and organizing school or neighborhood activities is another way working mothers have been placed aside. Mothers who work are forced by this action to depend on mothers who do not work.

The use of innuendos can also serve to "put working mothers in their place" or covertly "get even." Suggestions are dropped deliberately that working mothers might be having trouble with their children even though the children are well adjusted. Remarks are phrased to plant seeds of doubt in the mind of the working mother by others who will not accept the success such a mother can attain through her combination of professional and personal joys.

Women in "Male Jobs"

Another form of social restriction is imposed on mothers who work in predominantly male professions. The feeling is obvious, though unspoken, that the male network will not easily invite a working mother to join even though she may be a colleague. Wives of these men are even less accepting of women who work with their husbands as colleagues. Being one of the few female executives or female pioneers in a male company has its drawbacks in social restrictions. Not only do the men resent the intrusion of a female into the male club, the normal sexist struggle, but also their wives resent the time that a female spends with their husbands. As a result, the female worker feels isolated on the job and off.

Most of the men will abide by their instincts to remain apart from "her." Some of them are under strict orders from home not to socialize with "that woman in your office" even if she happens to be the boss. It is also true that wives feel quite threatened by a working woman, especially by a well-organized mother who shows she really "has her act together" and manages her life well. The working mother may overshadow the man's wife who stays home and doesn't seem as organized, as up-to-date, or as knowledgeable in comparison.

An exception to the negative wife is the older wife who is beyond childcare responsibilities and will often see the working mother as her own daughter. She can support the efforts of a diligent working mother. One basic criterion for acceptance by the older or more experienced woman is that she has attained some measure of success and happiness throughout her own life. Without this, she probably will not have the sympathetic or caring feelings to extend to a working mother.

A few men will show interest socially in the working mother—for various reasons. There are those men who are seeking the obvious sexual favors and will befriend any female, executive or clerical, offering their much-sought-after Don Juan services. There are also those men who will act friendly but will not be sincere. They see this new working mother in the office as temporary and vulnerable. She is a prime target for their attentions. Social gestures of such men are inconsistent and geared toward their own perceptions of payoff.

Then again, there are those men who are secure about their positions and self-confident about their own abilities. These men will be friendly to any deserving colleague, regardless of sex. They have no motivation outside sincerity and goal achievement. Many working women find this category of men to be composed primarily of single men, but this may not always be the case. Men in this category don't even mind hearing about a woman's children, provided, of course, she doesn't go beyond reason.

LIVING WITH YOUR CHOICES

For years, women have worked because they had to, either to support a family or to assure a certain standard of living. Working mothers have had problems long before the women's movement helped to clarify those problems. Prior to that time the situation of a working mother and her conflicts was viewed as unfortunate.

In *A Guide for Working Mothers,* Jean Curtis stated that working mothers are suspected of radicalism as well as neglect. The women's movement heightened that prejudice through public awareness about changes in the roles of women and brought fear about the gradual erosion of the traditional housewife and the nuclear family.

Women feel more scrutinized than they have in the past. Male disapproval of working mothers is expected, whereas female disapproval causes working mothers to feel defensive and angry. It is more difficult to prove proper parenting than professional competence. Many women simply believe it is wrong to combine work and motherhood and these beliefs are channeled into actions through words and deeds which make the life of a working mother even more difficult. Problems with children of working mothers are the same as those of mothers who stay home, yet mothers who work are in many subtle ways made to feel "I told you so" about working.

Mothers think a great deal about the consequences of working on their children. They are made to feel a series of conflicts: guilt, stress, pressure, and social restrictions. They are asked to combine two full-time jobs into only one full-time day. And what is asked of their children or the fathers of those children? Often little or nothing is offered to support her efforts. Every situation, of course, is different and what works for one person through scheduling or supportive assistance may not work for another. However, the basic premise has been that in too many cases the woman allows herself to feel negatively about the working situation when she could often turn it around to a more positive one.

Many women simply are hesitant to shift or share child-rearing responsibilities. They are afraid that "only a mother can know." This is not only unnecessary, it is selfish. A relationship built on trust and love is not threatened by anyone else, by time spent with sitters or by innuendoes of jealous but, of course, well-meaning friends. It is selfish because mothers are using their children to fulfill every aspect of their life, to be in actuality, an extension of themselves, still dependent on that umbilical cord for sustenance. Mothers should carefully assess their actions and determine if they are really perpetuating passive dependence or if they are providing experiences for growth and the development of independence.

Children are more versatile and more adaptable than many mothers realize or want to admit. Mothers who can step back and help their children develop independence can usually view their children's behavior and development with a greater degree of objectivity than a mother who maintains dependence or remains with her children all the time.

The children of working mothers learn delayed gratification since they usually must wait until the mother comes home for praise and solace. Working mothers are told more about their children from different sources than nonworking mothers and they seem to be able to keep communication open toward certain goals the child is working to achieve. In addition, they have the time away to recapitulate and make decisions on actions to be taken.

Nonworking mothers, on the other hand, tend to react quickly and without reflection. Even though they have the time to stop and think, they do not always do it. In addition, after spending many hours with the children, they may not have the patience necessary for the situation.

Working mothers have a unique opportunity for teaching. They can utilize the time that children have at home without their mother's presence to develop responsibilities. The acceptance of responsibility is, as educators say, a transferable skill of learning. That is, a child who *learns* that he is expected to clean up the kitchen and dust the family room before his mother comes home at 5:00 P.M. can usually be depended on to bring his papers to school on time and prepare assignments on schedule. Praise from his mother upon her arrival will reinforce cooperative behavior. An appeal to the team effort of working together will also initiate cooperation while serving to stop the continuation of the myth that all home responsibilities are to be taken care of by the mother.

Most working mothers learn to handle conflicts once they have made the decision to combine a career with motherhood. Very few fail if they carefully recognize the pitfalls of guilt, stress, restrictions, and lack of support. Working mothers must realize these confrontations have been cast on women for decades, and the woman's movement has caused the conflict to be open for scrutiny in the full view of contemporary society.

Most women who make the choice to work do so because they have recognized needs and talents within themselves which they want to pursue. The development of each woman as an individual to the fullest capacity of her strengths and talents is not only natural but also a phenomenon of life which has been until recently overlooked. Restrictions imposed by traditions have only served to limit and frustrate talented women. Women as a resource have been underdeveloped by nations which have failed to examine the full potential of their populations.

Women who choose to work not only contribute the talents of their minds and hands to the work force of the nation but also contribute to the economy of the nation as well.

Most women in this category consider themselves to have the best of both worlds even though they have to fight prejudice against being where they are. The self-satisfaction of developing one's abilities and enjoying the rewards of one's work, as men have always been allowed to do, far outweighs the trials and tribulations of conflict. Women thrive on the variety and richness they can choose in their lives thanks to the degree of independence achieved by working. Their life cord no longer must be attached to a male for survival, socially or economically. Very few women feel their lives would be more satisfying if they quit working. Those who are left in the quagmire of unhappiness or indecision can usually be helped by a careful analysis of choices and priorities. Often, the dissatisfaction stems from elements of the job and is not a reflection on working. Yet some women may not have clarified this issue and are in a state of confusion over their negative, ambivalent, or indifferent feelings about career and family. They are unable to define the source of their unrest. Often a realistic comparison of the alternatives for their lives will assist in this clarification process. A woman must be committed to the sense of inner satisfaction and independence derived from working and must know how to organize to get the most from each day, week, and month in order to achieve the satisfaction she desires. Without this planning, organizing, and recognizing the inherent negatives against working mothers, women will continue to face the same emotional conflicts brought to bear in the past.

Some mothers seem almost to enjoy the martyrdom of the restricted life placed on them by the needs of their children. Women such as these make sure that others know of their plight, which is correlated with being a successful mother. Sacrifice equates with motherhood to some women.

Another vulnerable period for working mothers involves various stages of development or stressful periods in the lives of their children. As children grow up, they experience varied problems and crises which seem insurmountable at the time. However, for children the crises are real and the children are quite disturbed. Working mothers often shoulder the blame for these shaky periods in the lives of their children. Talking and sharing with other mothers whose children have experienced that stage of development can be most helpful to mothers going through a new series of crises.

Many working mothers consistently feel at fault for something that bothers their children. In some instances, they may be right, but few children can be raised to adulthood without passing through periods of stress, whether or not the mother is at home all the time. Children need more than anything to know that they are loved and cared for and that their parents (whether one or two) are available and accessible to them.

Positive thinking helps to arm working mothers against extreme reactions. This strengthens a working mother and helps guard against any negative feelings which tend to repress the natural satisfaction experienced as a result of working. Needs of children vary according to stages of development and stimuli to which they are exposed. Some problems are of course more serious than others, and solutions may not be simple. A mother who is able to feel confident about satisfying the needs of her children has an advantage in handling periods of stress and crisis. For the insecure mother, these kinds of problems grow intense, often without justification. Working mothers sometimes lack the confidence and security needed to be emotionally well equipped for problem solving. Assessment of individual situations can often be inaccurate. Mothers feel trapped between their own guilt of working and the problems experienced by their children. This emotional confusion makes clarification of problems and solutions difficult. A mother caught in her own sea of guilt and confusion can expect difficulty in most situations that arise whether major or minor in importance. A mother who is self-assured about her choices, however, is more likely to assume that problems are temporary and can be resolved soon. Such mothers have learned to balance their time with the flexibility required to fulfill their children's needs and their own. Serious problems take more time to solve and require a greater amount of output from a mother's time. However, children have been known to make inhuman demands on a working mother, and a perceptive and confident mother can readily recognize those instances.

Feedback from another qualified person often helps solve a child's problems. Many times the blame for a particular problem is placed on the mother's employment or the home situation. Solving the problem from this set of assumptions may not get to the source of the child's problem. Conflicts can arise from undetected learning difficulties, peer pressure, lack of self-worth, or teasing. All of these can cause children to experience difficulties in a classroom and none are directly attributable to a mother's working. Any number of professionally trained people can assist in giving an outside opinion without bias against a working mother. Unbiased opinions are important since many people, including some professionals, have an antagonistic attitude toward working mothers. Getting sound advice about childhood adjustment problems is essential and will lead to a more accurate plan for resolution. Working mothers may have to make an extra effort to show professionals who work with their children that they are as concerned and loving as other mothers. Some teachers are especially guilty in this regard even though they may be working mothers themselves.

The attitude of some doctors and counselors toward mothers who work is a dictate of their own morals and values rather than being based on sound research. Some of these professionals openly disapprove of mothers being absent from the home and in so doing produce added guilt to that already felt by the mothers. The advice they give, however, is usually not widely supported by research.

Coping with problems is notably easier for working mothers who possess the confidence necessary for detachment. Some women are able to exchange ideas and feelings with a reassuring husband. Others, perhaps divorced or widowed, do not have such access. For these women, coping is usually more difficult, but they can depend on their own strength and common sense.

Children often sense conflict if it is present in the home. When conflict is within a mother's mind, she should be careful not to transfer it to the child. Children can sense tension, whether verbal or nonverbal, related to a mother's work. Family arguments rub off on children, who feel conflict and confusion. Their imaginations may cause them to feel frightened or isolated about their mother's disappearance.

Explaining to children a few simple details about what their mother does at work or taking them to visit the place of employment can help alleviate such fears. Children can hang pictures they have drawn on their mother's walls as a reminder of them while she works. A mother needs to feel secure enough about her choice to work in order to display the pictures because such art demonstrates pride in her children to others and underscores the fact to colleagues that she is a working mother. Employers might consider the idea of an "open house" at Christmas or various holidays especially for the children of those who work there.

Women who are dissatisfied with their jobs will have difficulty solving problems at home. Their own psychological stress compounds the problems.

Getting out into the world of work is exciting for many women. They experience a combination of roles: earth mother, professional dedicated worker, friend, lover, wife. They dare to dream thoughts and goals, long forgotten by others.

Once the decisions have been made and the conflict faced, mothers, fathers, and children can mold their lives with a bond of enrichment. They can each look forward to the end of the day—to coming home and seeing the people they really care about. Running a house is not just a matter of cut-and-dried schedule or a list of who does what chore. It is much more. A home and family is an artful blend of needs, feelings, responsibilities, and fulfillment for the family as a unit. Far from breaking down the family unit, the working mother can serve as a catalyst for teaching children to give and take, to trust and love, to work and earn rewards—and that is what most parents aim to achieve in life anyway.

8
Conflict and Choice: A Summary

SOCIETY SENDS conflicting messages to women. The family is held as a priority, yet the value of monetary positions is also seen as worthwhile. Today most women who have chosen to work outside the home do so because they need the money. In the past, women have been asked to consider working in time of war or inflation, to meet the family needs by augmenting the income, or to fill time after the children are grown. The motivation given to women was based on contingencies predicated on the needs of others—not on women themselves. Women have progressed from living for the needs of others to fulfilling their own. However, there are inherent conflicts for a woman who struggles to combine family and career.

Attitudes frequently lag behind realities. In trying to live with the traditions of yesteryear, changes often remain unrecognized. A changing society can prompt frustration and self-doubt among its members. Social conflicts can significantly increase when a substantial component does not receive just compensation or recognition. Women have felt isolated, misinterpreted, and unrewarded by the present changing social system.

The twentieth-century emergence of the American woman from the status she historically held is a phenomenon dramatically illustrated in census bureau data. More women work than do not work. They work for a variety of reasons, but the primary reasons are financial. The trained career woman can no longer afford to drop out of work. The working woman has become a norm as much as the mother who stayed home in the past.

It is time for motherhood to be transformed from its narrow image to a broader, more realistic concept. Just as women have an equal right to a career, men have an obligation to share in childcare. Although the role of mother produces many demands, rewarding and unrewarding, the role per se need not mean a life of sacrifice. Women are continuing to struggle to meet those demands and expand their own lives. In the process, they are confronted with conflict from every direction. However, as the understanding of both women and men increase about the expanding roles of women and the necessity for change, the predictable conflicts can perhaps be diminished.

Change in attitude is difficult for many men and women to achieve. They may want to expand their horizons about the roles of women but may not be able to because of an extremely traditional background. Many find the replacement of one role for another a hard task. The work force is very competitive, and the characteristics needed to survive are in direct opposition to many of those needed to maintain a colleagial partnership at home. Cooperation in the home is hard to achieve when one is geared toward the competitive world of work. Aggressive traits have to be cast off and a new role begun. Both men and women who fail to make this change successfully bring additional conflicts into the home. If children are part of the family, they interpret the conflict as an insecure environment—one of striving rather than cooperating.

A woman needs practical support and emotional support just as a man does. Practical support comes in the form of relieving the struggle of women to live two lives. Relief of daily tasks that have been "assigned" to women and an agreed on division of labor can help to alleviate some of the struggles women face.

Women can and do achieve the same degrees of satisfaction from a career as their male counterparts. The centrality of that career, can be challenged with the birth of the first child. Many women postpone the decision in order to have both career and children, yet the event can have a different meaning than expected. Some career women are incredibly delighted with the experience of motherhood. Others are overwhelmed with the physical and emotional impact and find it quite different from what they had anticipated.

As for women who choose to combine both worlds, the social system can indirectly help them achieve a balance. Professional women may be excused from activities in various organizations because people realize they may be overextended. However, some working mothers refuse to allow this. They insist on fulfilling every possible obligation attached to each role in order to prove they are not negligent in personal or professional performance. Without limits on the allocation of time and strength, a working mother may experience conflict and tension.

Those who postpone having a career and a family may experience as much difficulty orchestrating both as did women who had children without planning years in advance. Usually, women who postpone children are well-planned perfectionists with very high standards. The new experience is a continuous compromise which can extend women, especially those without the support discussed, in several directions, often in excess of their resources. The idea of competence and the multiplicity of commitments may be overloaded.

Women experiencing such conflict may be failing to see the change that has occurred. They are continuing to see themselves as they were with added dimensions. However, they need to redefine themselves by standards of parenthood rather than narrowly to judge themselves only through their pursuit of work.

One theory about working mothers is that they have stronger identities because of their increased responsiveness to others, which comes through the heightened sensitivity of motherhood. The tolerance level for stress and stamina increase. Women learned how to compromise and how to sacrifice in the past. They have been manipulated and controlled by others. This experience has not suppressed their desire to achieve. They have learned how to turn quiet compromise into a strength. Women are changing from being submissive to powerful in the control of their lives.

Norris and Miller stated in the *Working Mother's Complete Handbook* that working can be a satisfying endeavor and make a woman a different, fuller person.

> *When a woman can drag from her experience of mothering feelings that overflow and make her a more confident worker, she realizes a dream that all of us have; to unite the worlds of love and work; to joint seamlessly the purely individual needs that each of us carries throughout life along with the needs of our family; to balance our powerful complex of demands so that neither robs the other and we*

can better enjoy both halves of the full human person—caring and achieving. An elusive marriage, but one worth working and fighting for.[1]

Motherhood is only one part of the process of womanhood, and it is now a choice, not an inevitable event. It is not an identity for all women. It is a choice—an additional part of a full and satisfying life already established by previous choices. Motherhood is not an escape. The choice can lead to the serenity of fulfillment though mixed with a sense of power and powerlessness. It is the process of giving life and receiving life anew. It is exhilaration and exhaustion simultaneously. More than anything else, motherhood is a choice to enter an intense reciprocal relationship.

Choices exist for women, but choices of one degree or another have always existed. Earlier, the choice was between becoming a career woman or becoming a mother. The major change facing women or later generations is that choices are being made by all women and the choices do not always complement each other. There are no longer "traditional" paths which go unquestioned. There are no more majority decisions for women. No matter which direction a woman chooses for her life, there is potential for conflict.

As women continue to make choices and to struggle with the conflicts of those choices, they learn to utilize whatever pragmatic methods are needed to implement their decisions. Their lives may not always be free of conflict, but their decision reflects a commitment to the choice nevertheless.

The time is past wherein women carried overwhelming guilt for determining their own priorities. Women do not have to put their needs and interests last and continue in the submissive role of bygone days. Women have the opportunity to develop self-awareness and discover their potential talents, whatever they happen to be. They must mold new visions of themselves and realistically consider women as serious contributors to the family income and the work force. With such expanded visions, women can enjoy increased career opportunities and take pride in the development of their abilities. After all, talent and leadership can easily be hidden in unsuspecting packages. Without the potential contributions of women, the nation is only half developed.

Conflict does not have to lead to frustration and stress. It can be an

---

[1]Gloria Norris and Jo Ann Miller, *The Working Mother's Complete Handbook* (New York: E.P. Dutton, 1979), p. 199.

opportunity to grow. By working through conflict, women and men can clarify their own understanding of their actions, weigh the possible consequences in light of each situation, and make an informed decision.

A major factor in feeling successful and happy is having the confidence that the decisions you chose to make were the right ones for a particular set of circumstances. It is a waste of psychological energy to spend time reflecting on whether past decisions were wise.

A woman should have the opportunity to decide, without pressure or guilt, among every alternative open to her. If she wants to be a full-time homemaker, that's fine, if she enjoys it. A woman must freely enter into her commitments rather than feel bound to a certain course by relatives or an unexpectedly narrow-minded mate. Otherwise, she will resent the direction of her life and eventually rebel in frustration manifested overtly or covertly.

Most women hope that their daughters will have the same opportunities for choices as their sons. Why shouldn't they? A female in this contemporary, changing society has every right to be a free person, a free woman who is able to experience life as she chooses.

Index